Praise for *Propel*

"Whitney deftly describes the full spectrum of strategies and tactics available to today's savvy marketers, including how and when to use them and—just as importantly—when *not* to. The host of practical tips and real-world examples she shares will allow anyone to sharpen their marketing approach to more effectively engage customers and drive bottom-line results."

—Caroline Boren, managing director of Loyalty Marketing and Customer Advocacy for Alaska Airlines

"In our marketing-saturated culture, finding new ways to get your message heard is increasingly difficult. Fortunately, with this book, Whitney provides many practical, manageable, and effective methods for making marketing work for your business. It is a great read and reflects the author's passion and expertise."

—Norman Guadagno, managing director, Wire Stone

"In *Propel*, Whitney Keyes does what few business authors manage to do: make marketing accessible and results-driven for busy change-makers who are tired of theoretical concepts that fail to attract customers, reach goals, or increase revenue. In her practical and punchy way, she focuses readers on clear action steps and offers fantastic real-world case studies to bring her points home. This book will spark ideas for anyone from a Main Street store owner to a Fortune 500 marketing executive. Wake up, business gurus: Keyes is the new experienced voice in town, offering a fresh, practical guide that turns strategy into real results."

—Maria Ross, creator of and chief strategist for Red Slice, and author of *Branding Basics for Small Business*

"*Propel* is like a breezy lunch conversation about how to promote a business, generously sprinkled with case studies, quotes, and anecdotes. These stories clearly illustrate well-known marketing principles and serve them up in easily digestible bites. The chapters on extending your reach through the media and partnerships alone make this book worth the read."

—Robbin Block, marketing strategist, "Minding Your Business" host, public speaker, and author of *Social Persuasion*

"If you want fanatical fans and evangelist customers, you absolutely must read this book. Whitney lays out the proven formula used by break-through startups and the biggest corporations on earth. A must-read for every entrepreneur."

—Joe Abraham, founder of bosiDNA.com and author of *Entrepreneurial DNA*

"Whitney distills complex marketing concepts into easy-to-apply ideas that make the reader want to jump into action with their marketing! Chock full of examples and know-how, *Propel* guides the reader to zero in on the marketing activities that will build the business, and to confidently know what would be a waste of time."

—Juliet Sander, marketing instructor at the University of Washington, and founder of Sander Brand Culture

"Whitney Keyes has created the blueprint for marketing success. *Propel* arms and empowers every businessperson with the tools, tactics, and action-able plans to accelerate their marketing efforts. She has done a phenomenal job at giving the reader clarity on how to implement proven processes to help them with their marketing dilemma. I agree 100 percent with Whitney in that 'marketing never stops'; everyone is in one business...the business of marketing. This book is concise and gets to the point. Marketing is not a 'spectator sport'; you have to be in the game and on the field with a plan and a playbook. *Propel* provides you with everything you need to win in today's fast-paced marketing game. Buy it, read it, and then take massive action to *propel* your marketing efforts and your bank account!"

—Eric Taylor, founder and chief collaboration officer of Eric Taylor Consulting Group and best-selling author of *Mastering the World of Selling*

"No matter what business you are in and what marketing strategy you have or have not committed to, Whitney brilliantly covers all the bases, outlining practical step-by-step tools and offering insightful case studies to show you what you can do to accelerate your business. The engaging modular structure allows you to move around in the book and find what is relevant to you. The 'Marketing Mindset' questions at the end of each chapter provide clear and concise summaries, inspiring you to turn realizations into tangible action steps. I highly recommend *Propel* to anyone who wants to develop and market their brand."

—Angela Heise, integrative trainer and coach

"This book brings clarity to the questions about branding and marketing and tie nicely to Law of Likability #1—the law of authenticity. In her book she takes a collaborative approach to getting ahead by teaming up with everyone from customers and competitors to the media."

—Michelle Tillis Lederman, author of *The 11 Laws of Likability* and CEO of Executive Essentials

"As an organizing and productivity expert, I love that Propel is full of simple, effective, easy to implement action steps. Marketing often overwhelms me, but this book walks me though everything I need to know with very relatable stories. I can't wait to implement these principles!"

—Stacey Anderson, publisher of *Getting Organized* magazine

PROPEL

FIVE WAYS TO
AMP UP YOUR MARKETING
AND ACCELERATE BUSINESS

WHITNEY KEYES

**Foreword by Maggie Winkel,
Director of Merchandising for Nike, Inc.**

CAREER
PRESS

Pompton Plains, N.J.

Copyright © 2012 by Whitney Keyes

PROPEL

EDITED AND TYPESET BY KARA KUMPEL

Cover design by Wes Youssi/M80 Branding

Printed in the U.S.A.

To order this title, please call toll-free 1-800-CAREER-1 (NJ and Canada: 201-848-0310) to order using VISA or MasterCard, or for further information on books from Career Press.

The Career Press, Inc.
220 West Parkway, Unit 12
Pompton Plains, NJ 07444
www.careerpress.com

Library of Congress Cataloging-in-Publication Data

Keyes, Whitney.

Five ways to amp up your marketing and accelerate business / by Whitney Keyes ; foreword by Maggie Winkel.

      p. cm.

Includes bibliographical references and index.

ISBN 978-1-60163-233-3 -- ISBN 978-1-60163-578-5 (e-book) 1. Marketing. 2. Internet marketing. 3. Branding (Marketing). 4. Customer relations. I. Title.

    HF5415.K4643 2012
    658.8--dc23

                                             2012016829

To my incredible family and friends, wonderful colleagues, and all of the remarkable clients and students I've met over the years.

Acknowledgments

Acknowledging the good that you already have in your life is the foundation for all abundance.
—Eckhart Tolle

This book wouldn't be in your hands without a great deal of support and encouragement from many people. I'm especially grateful to the individuals I've named in every chapter who were willing to share their stories. Here are a few more people who helped me along the way to turn initial ideas into a final manuscript:

Absolutely essential: The Minas Keyes clan

Amazing agent: John Willig

Brilliant advisors: Stacey Anderson, Michael Brasky, Michael Coy, Michelle Craig, Elisabeth Dale, Barbie Hull, Waverly Fitzgerald, Peggy Fischer, Elaine Long, Barb Minas, Karri Patton, Angie Ramos, Maria Ross, Mayna Sgaramella McVey, Penny Whisler, Maggie Winkel, and Soon Beng Yeap

Career Press: Michael Pye, Laurie Kelly-Pye, Kirsten Dalley, Gina Talucci, Kara Kumpel, Jeff Piasky, and Wes Youssi (cover design), and everyone else who worked behind the scenes

Corporate agility: Alaska Airlines (Caroline Boren, Bobbie Egan, Kelli Goss, Darbie Kirk, Curtis Kopf, Paul McElroy, and Joe Sprague),

American Express (Sarah Meron, Patrick Jones), Microsoft (Stacey Drake McCredy and Lisa Stratton), and Starbucks (Alisa Martinez and Corey duBrowa)

Dynamic duos: Josh Keyes and Lisa Ericson, Steph and Rich Rowland, Liz and George Hatziantoniou, Tami Nassiri and Vassilis Chamalidis, Vani and Dash Dhakshinamoorthy, Adriana and Linda Suleiman, and last but by all means not least, Wyatt Bardouille and Jan Ostman

Eagle-eye editing: Ellen Kadin, Kerry Lehto, Shana McNally, Wylie O'Sullivan, and Nancy Wick

Essential ladies and gentlemen: Kristen Akyel, Ron Asahara, David Bovee, Michelle Buzzoni, Heather Correa, Lauren Davis, Karl Fjellström, Amy Goldstein, Gay Goodman, Shelby Gregg, Ann Guinn, Josh Holland, Larry Johnson, Karen Kershaw, David Kubiczky, George Meng, Susan Metters, Jon Misola, Barry Mitzman, Kini Parente, Kim Pearson, Marsha Perry, Molly Phillips, Susie Prets, Arissa Rench, Rey Sabado, Masae Rhoton, Albert Treskin, and Tamika Vinson

Good government types: Carol (Cha Cha) Andersen, George Beukes, Ellen Bienstock, Wing Foong Chew, Christine Clifford, George Gakuo, Halima Gichuki, Rozana Hanipah, Lisa Heilbronn, Sherry Mina, Yvonne Oh, Sadayan (Riaz) Riazurrahman, Gretchen Weintraub, and Nick Papp

Heart, mind, and soul: Barbara Rose Chateaubriand

Legal ease: Dan Waggoner

Multimedia crew: Brett Renville, Andy Lo, Androu Morgan (and "let there be cake" Barbara Fugate), and Vijay Sureshkumar

Photography: David Hiller

President of the fan club: Barry Ross Rinehart

Spare families: The Bardouilles, Ericsons, Nassiris, Pimentels, and Whitons

Sweetheart: Joel Shapiro

T-town roots: Les Barnett, Mariza Craig, Katy Jolley, Keith Stone, and Dan Voelpel

Unconditional love: Domino

Writer gals: Karen Burns, Michelle Goodman, Michelle Tillis Lederman, and Gail Martin

Contents

Foreword

by Maggie Winkel,
Director of Branding,
Nike, Inc.

FOREWORD

by Maggie Winkel, Director of Merchandising, Nike, Inc

IN MY 25 YEARS of professional experience I have enjoyed the good fortune of participating in and leading the furthering, developing, and redeveloping of some of the apparel industry's greatest brands: Levi Strauss, Macy's, GAP Inc., Ann Taylor LOFT, and Tommy Bahama. I've also had the pleasure of advising savvy entrepreneurs on their way to creating the next great brand, which brings me to how I met Whitney Keyes.

I was hosting a panel interview of marketing experts during an entrepreneurial exposition, and Whitney was on the panel. During the course of the discussion, Whitney's passion for marketing shone through—her responses were rooted in strategy, common sense, fun, and a do-it-yourself attitude, and the audience members were scrambling to capture what she was sharing. I was so impressed by Whitney and her unique approach to marketing that I reached out to her to collaborate on future consulting projects and business seminars, and we've been colleagues ever since.

Whitney's keen understanding that the challenges of running an organization of any size can keep you perpetually focused on working *in* your business instead of *on* your business has led her to enable business evolution and growth across a spectrum of influence: from leading teams inside giants such as Microsoft to being invited by the U.S. State Department to host workshops in Malaysia and Africa for women-owned start-ups. Whether she's delivering a keynote presentation in front of hundreds of entrepreneurs or lecturing to a university class, her philosophy and approach remains the same—use a simple, consistent, strategic approach to build a plan that is actionable—and propels your organization forward.

I recently referred a client to Whitney and saw the ideas she shares in this book come to life. The entrepreneur was producing a line of innovative, one-of-a-kind gift cards and was overwhelmed with places to begin her marketing activities. She was struggling to manage time staying on top of Facebook posts and writing articles for her blog and wasn't in a position yet to hire an expensive marketing agency. In just one conversation, Whitney helped the business owner bridge her long-term vision with her immediate need to generate more revenue. Whitney coached her on how to quickly get her product into the hands of influential buyers and boutique store owners and motivated her to create an internship position to get immediate marketing and PR help for free.

That brings me to why I love this book so much: it's because *Propel* is the next best thing to having Whitney on your team! It's straightforward, well-written, and makes taking the steps to building a meaningful and successful marketing plan that connects with consumers achievable. Whitney's "Five Principles" provide an elegant and effective framework that anyone can use to drive their business to new levels of success.

What's even better about having this book is that you can work through the principles in any order—whatever works best for your team—and use them at any time in a business lifecycle. In fact, organizations can return to them again and again, and continue to achieve positive results—whether simply refining their plan to be even more focused, building upon the work that was previously done to expand their brand reach, or even starting over with certain elements based on new learnings.

Generating fast, smart ideas that work and inspiring you to use them to get to the next level—that's Whitney in action, whether she's working with a Fortune 500 company or a nonprofit. I hope you enjoy reading *Propel* and use it to turn your ideas into action and achieve great success.

Maggie Winkel
director of merchandising,
Nike, Inc.

INTRODUCTION

FROM THE LATEST SOCIAL media campaigns to old-school publicity stunts and everything in between, marketing has the potential to positively transform your company. Because your organization is unique, there's a distinct formula of marketing activities key to its success. The good news is that marketing isn't like calculus. You'll never have to solve complex problems such as $F(x)\ dx = F(b)-F(a)$. Thank goodness for that. But it isn't overly simple like grade-school math, either; 2 plus 2 doesn't always equal 4 in the world of marketing. There is no one-size-fits-all answer. I've never seen someone create a perfectly designed customer satisfaction survey that guarantees 100 percent results every time, not to mention 100 percent positive feedback. It just isn't possible. But there is a process for creating the right marketing equation, needed to move your business forward so you can reach your goals.

In some ways, doing effective marketing is like putting together a puzzle. You try to assemble all the pieces you have to work with to match the picture on the cover of the box—your ideal result. But unlike puzzles you're familiar with, the pieces of the marketing puzzle can change during the process. For example, you might hold an annual fundraiser for your top 300 supporters, but the issues facing your organization today may not be the same as they were a year ago. You need to adapt to the current situation and refresh your marketing approach to ensure it's relevant and effective in enticing people to attend the event and motivating them to donate.

It's that challenge, that inability to know exactly how the marketing game will be played out that makes it so exciting and interesting. It can be a lot of fun, too. What other aspect of business lets you do things such as throw parties, design logos, order cool T-shirts, and share photos on Flickr? And one of the best things about marketing today is that the playing field has been leveled. Success isn't dependent on the size of your company or the amount of your budget. Size doesn't matter. Smart marketing does. And anyone can do it.

Take Kay Hirai, for example. She's an animal lover who heard about more than 600 dogs and puppies suffering in three puppy mills. All of the animal shelters in the region stepped up to save the dogs, including a small nonprofit called Ginger's Pet Rescue. But the dogs were in very poor health and desperately needed medical care before they could be put up for adoption. When Kay learned online that Ginger's was having trouble covering its escalating veterinarian bills and other expenses needed for the rehabilitation process, she stepped up to help.

In an effort to help the struggling shelter and save the dogs' lives, Kay decided to launch an all-out fundraising campaign. She recruited friends, clients, and the community to come to an event in her beauty salon, Studio 904. More than 100 people showed up to see 16 of the dogs, learn more about their dire situation, and help the cause. In just a few hours, they opened their hearts and their checkbooks and helped Kay raise more than $10,000 to go toward rescue expenses for the dogs in Ginger's care.

It's extremely easy these days for anyone to send a press release around the world, use Facebook to promote an event to 50,000 people, or even produce and post a video to YouTube. Each of these marketing activities can be done in a matter of minutes. And for those lacking tech-savvy abilities or with limited access to technology, there is still an abundance of offline marketing activities to choose from to help move your business forward.

MARKETING MISTAKES

But even with all of these powerful tools and techniques at your disposal, some people still make marketing mistakes. They waste precious time, money, and resources doing activities that don't work. I've seen an entrepreneur spend a fortune on a customized Website, only to be left scratching his head, wondering why he experienced no direct boost in online traffic. Big corporations make marketing blunders, too. Groupon spent millions on a TV ad campaign for the Super Bowl that offended many of the more than 100 million people who saw it. The daily discount coupon company did the right thing and quickly pulled the ads and followed up with a public apology from its CEO.[1] But by then, the marketing budget was spent and the damage was done. The week after the Super Bowl, game-day commercials from other advertisers including GoDaddy.com and Volkswagen directly led to Website traffic upwards of 41 percent from unique visitors.[2] But Groupon didn't fare so well. Its Website traffic increased by a measly 3 percent.

So, yes, anyone *can* do marketing, but true success lies in *how* you do marketing. How can you use the tools in the most effective ways to get the right results that move you closer to your goals? I'll never forget a woman who attended one of the social media seminars I delivered for the Small Business Administration. As the session began, she raised her hand and said, "I hate to admit this, but I feel like I'm so behind the times. I haven't done any marketing yet and I know I need to be doing more with Twitter, but I have no clue where to begin." Before I started explaining the tweeting process, I asked for more details about her business. It turned out she had spent most of her career as a geriatric nurse, and in the past year, decided to start her own business providing in-home elder care for senior citizens. She had no clear marketing plan and lacked a solid base of clients. On the surface, she thought her customers were seniors in their 80s and 90s with disabilities—in which case it wouldn't have made sense for her to use Twitter to reach them. But her thinking was mistaken in a second way: She hadn't yet thought about the fact that it's often the adult children who influence their aging parents' decisions about personal care. In any event, social media was not going to help much at this early phase of her business.

I ended up talking her out of spending a lot of time learning about Twitter and encouraged her to begin forming partnerships with senior centers, medical clinics, and local hospitals. Professionals there would likely value her expertise and might be willing to let her hold information sessions for the people they served. Once they had seen her in action, they would be in a position to refer potential clients to her immediately. Without a basic understanding of what marketing is and how it works, it's easy to make the kind of mistake this woman in my seminar made.

Where many people get tripped up with their marketing is not in their ability to do it, but in their knowledge about it. In fact, according to the U.S. Small Business Administration, one of the top 10 reasons businesses fail is a lack of basic information about effective marketing.[3] This clearly holds true for larger companies as well. In a recent study of senior marketing leaders at Fortune 100 and Forbes Top 200 corporations, only 11 percent of these executives consider their organizations "very effective" at marketing, especially when it comes to integrating new tools such as social media into their existing strategies.[4] Here are five of the common marketing mistakes I've seen organizations make.

1. Being Impatient

I can't tell you how many times I've heard something along these lines: "I sent my press release to 20 TV reporters yesterday, but I never heard back from any of them. I guess they weren't interested." Or this: "I spent hours writing my blog article and not one person commented on it." We do live in a culture based on instant gratification. But as I mentioned earlier, marketing is an unpredictable game. You never know exactly what will work and precisely when you'll see the results.

I once heard back from a reporter a year after I sent an e-mail pitch. I was working for a client in the sporting goods industry and we were trying to get national print outlets such as *Men's Health* and *Outside* magazine to write positive reviews of the product line. The journalist told me he thought the news idea was great, but that he had filed it away for a rainy day when he couldn't come up with his own angle for a story.

Giving up too soon in the marketing process doesn't get you very far; sometimes, being patient and taking just a bit more time can pay off in a very big way. That said, this book is all about quick results, so if your marketing isn't working, you've got to know when to cut bait and move on. I certainly didn't wait around for that journalist to reply and continued to work hard to get my client results through other media outlets.

2. Overachieving

Twitter and Facebook and Yelp, oh my! Some people think they need to be doing everything and anything to promote their companies. Desperately seeking the secret to marketing nirvana, they try a little—or a lot—of everything. They try every tool their colleagues are talking about and jump on every new trend in the news. They randomly produce videos for YouTube, hold one event after another, create an online contest, revamp the Website, offer discounts, and the list goes on. Like a kid in a candy shop or my grandfather at the buffet table, they overdo it. Their approach is scattered, and, in trying to do so much, they get spread too thin and don't feel so good when their endless efforts don't get results.

You often need to use different marketing techniques to reach the right audiences, but that doesn't mean you should go every which way. It pays to have a method to help manage what could end up being marketing madness. It may seem counterintuitive, but when faced with a major business challenge, instead of throwing too much wood onto the fire, the real solution often lies in carefully choosing the *right* wood and placing it in the right formation to fuel your marketing efforts. Success doesn't come from doing *more activities*; it happens when you do the *right activities well*.

3. Obsessing

Another mistake people often make is putting all of their eggs into one marketing basket. Too often they get obsessed with a trendy new tool or technique and focus in on the wrong marketing tool. It's easy to do but you want to avoid having an obsessive-compulsive relationship with your marketing. One of my clients calls this the "crow syndrome": She looks for the shiniest object—whatever activity is closest, easiest, or most fun—and does it first. Social media is at the top of the obsession list right now. Many companies think it's the absolute best way to reach people. It isn't. According to a recent Gallup poll of almost 20,000 social media users, corporate social media may be the least effective way of influencing customers' opinions, especially people new to your products and services.[5] People are far more likely to rely on personal recommendations from family and friends.

Sure, tools such as Twitter and Pinterest, the newest social media darling, are important to consider and certainly easy to use. But they are just two pieces of the ever-changing marketing puzzle. For some organizations, it might make sense to invest a significant portion of marketing activities into Pinterest, but for others, it might not make any sense at all. What's most important is finding the right combination of marketing tools and techniques to help you effectively connect to your clients. Remember, it's not about what you want to do, it's about what works for them.

4. Getting Overwhelmed

And then there are the people with the best intentions. They want to do more marketing. They have crystal-clear goals, an impressive to-do list, and even all the right research to show what they should be doing, but they can't get one foot out of the gate. They are overwhelmed by all the marketing options and different tools and don't know where to start. Some people were born with procrastination in their blood. They enjoy the process of weighing the pros and cons and analyzing the entire situation before them. Even when it comes to e-mailing a follow-up note to customers, they just can't seem to hit that Send button. There's never enough time in the day. But if you spend too much time looking down, carefully watching each step on your way to the perfect moment, it just might pass you by. I've seen a lot of people hold back on marketing, which ultimately prevents their business from making good progress.

5. Being Overconfident

I hear this from a lot from the entrepreneurs I work with, especially startups and small business owners. Don't get me wrong; they've often done a good job of covering the basics. They have a solid business plan, a stack of spiffy business cards in hand, a functioning Website, and a really cool logo. "I have enough customers," they often say. "Why should I invest any time or money in marketing?" They think they can rest on their laurels and cross marketing completely off of their to-do list. I take a different approach. I think marketing works best when it's an ongoing part of your business and constantly integrated into everything you do. In truth, your marketing is never completely done.

▮▶   ▮▶   ▮▶

All of these common mistakes demonstrate why it's so important to get as much information up front as possible about what marketing is and how to do it in a more efficient way. It makes a tremendous difference in whether or not you'll be successful. A perfect place to start is the American Marketing Association's Website, where you'll find a definition for *marketing* along these lines:

> "the activity, set of institutions, and processes for creating, communicating, delivering, and exchanging offerings that have value for customers, clients, partners, and society at large."[6]

This is certainly a comprehensive and accurate explanation. But to make my point, consider this much more simplified definition of marketing that 95 percent of the participants in my seminars give when I ask them to explain the term:

> the act of promoting your product or service.

From a flier you post on a coffee shop bulletin board to a customer testimonial you post on your corporate Website, and even your e-mail signature and voice mail—all of these tools have marketing potential.

From building celebrity brands such as Oprah Winfrey's to boosting corporate identities such as Disney's, marketing creates tremendous possibilities, and when used correctly, can influence people's hearts and minds as well as their credit-card-holding hands. That's why my definition of marketing is all about turning basic communication efforts into more *strategic* activities:

planned activities that *accurately* promote a product, service, or information to an *intended* audience.

In the good old days, marketing was primarily used as a sales tool. It was a means to an end and you used it to do whatever was needed to move products and secure more customers. Fill your quota, and sell, sell, sell! Just watch any episode of the popular TV show *Mad Men* and you'll see what I mean. Numbers were the driving force in measuring an organization's success and holding marketing accountable. But today there is much more to marketing and much more of an emphasis on creating connections with customers through what's called *relationship marketing*. Just as environmentalists have been labeled "tree huggers," you could easily say we're in an era of "customer huggers." Using marketing to create the right customer experience is crucial to any organization's success.

Responsibility is also an important element in marketing today. Consumers expect organizations to be honest about their intentions and transparent in their actions. Marketing isn't just about making a profit; it's about making a positive impact on the community, and, in some cases, the environment. Most global corporations are evolving toward creating and communicating ethical standards across all aspects of their business practices, including their marketing activities.

Although times have changed, far too many organizations are still playing the old numbers-only game. By only focusing on the amount of Twitter followers or how many comments they get on a blog post, too little emphasis is given to the quality of the marketing campaign and a true relationship with those engaged customers. As a result, opportunities are often missed.

THE BIG MARKETING MASH-UP:
ADVERTISING, BRANDING, AND PR

When you get right down to it, marketing is action. Mastering your marketing is like having access to a big bucket of things you can do that have tremendous potential to help move your business forward. Some of those include sales activities, pricing structures, packaging, advertising campaigns, distribution methods, and media relations. From the over-arching process to the actual tools and techniques, marketing can easily become one big jumble in everyone's mind. People often confuse advertising, branding, and PR (public relations) with marketing. For this reason, I'll briefly clarify these terms and techniques to ensure we're on common ground. I'll go into some of them in much more detail later in the book, but for now, here's a quick look at what they are and how they differ from one another.

Marketing vs. Advertising

If marketing is an action, an ad is a specific tool you can use to perform the act. It's just one of many things you can do to reach your desired customers, audience, target market—whatever you want to call them. You use an ad to grab the attention of the people you want to reach. Depending on which type of advertisement you place (TV, Website, newspaper, billboard, and so on), those people might be viewers, readers, or listeners. In some cases, marketing might be free, such as when one of your customers says something positive about you to a friend—what's called word-of-mouth marketing. But *advertising* is almost always purchased. That means you have 99.9 percent control of your paid-for ad. For example, if you decide to place a print ad in your local business journal, you know exactly what size the ad will be, what the ad will say, what issue it will be in, and possibly even on what page it will appear. Advertising is just one part of the broad mix of marketing tools you can choose to use.

Marketing vs. Branding

If marketing is an action, and an ad is a tool, branding is more of an impression or sensation. A brand is the comprehensive experience you create through your marketing activities and tools that influences how your customers think, feel, and behave in response to your product or service. It's the unique personality of the organization that can—and should—be reflected in every one of your marketing activities. For a company such as Starbucks, branding goes far beyond just the infamous mermaid logo. In the company's retail spaces alone, the brand is communicated through everything from the music playing in the background to the paint on the walls and even the type of soap and toilet paper used in the restroom. An effective brand guides everything you do and impacts every marketing choice you make. I'll talk in much more detail about branding in Chapter 3.

Marketing vs. Public Relations (PR)

Unlike an ad, which is paid for, PR is often considered a free tool because it involves getting publicity for your organization in the form of a news story, not a paid advertisement. From a press release to a publicity stunt, PR can help you manage the flow of information and share messages with the public. PR is all about communicating in the most strategic way, using the art of persuasion and power of promotion to create, maintain, or restore an organization's image and reputation. In Chapter 7, I'll talk in more detail about how you can work with the media and use PR to help strengthen your marketing activities.

THE FIVE PRINCIPLES

As I said before, there is no one-size-fits-all answer to every organization's unique marketing dilemma. But there is a rock-solid approach that works like a charm every time. It doesn't matter if you're trying to get more customers to an in-store event or to spend time on your Website, this process will help you gain traction, get great results, and move you forward in the right direction.

Early in my career, I worked as a senior marketing manager for Microsoft at a time when some considered the company at the height of its success. My jobs were in a variety of groups, doing everything from launching $8 billion products to counseling Bill Gates for a *Wall Street Journal* interview. My teams managed multimillion-dollar budgets and developed global marketing programs at a time when the company had roughly 90,000 employees, close to 100 products, and $40 billion in revenue.

Since then, I've had the good fortune to work with organizations of all sizes, in every phase of development, and across just about every industry. I've helped Fortune 500 companies such as American Express, nonprofits such as the Sarawak Development Institute in Malaysia, and even a businesswoman who sold slivers of soap in Kibera, one of the world's largest slums. After talking with thousands of organizations around the world, the one thing I've found they all have in common is this: They need marketing solutions that work quickly and help them progress.

For almost a decade now, I've developed a core set of marketing principles and applied them to nonprofits, corporations, small businesses, schools—anyone interested in getting results. Success for any organization boils down to these five principles:

1. Strategy
2. Story
3. Strength
4. Simplicity
5. Speed

By using them together, you'll unlock your marketing potential and reveal new opportunities every time.

Principle 1. Strategy: Set Your Course for Success

Marketing can be incredibly fun and creative, but at the end of the day, it needs to be smart and well-directed. The problem is, too often people come up with a lot of great ideas, but then don't prioritize their marketing activities and end up spreading their efforts too thin. This first principle is all about helping you think before you act. In this section of the book, Part I, I'll help you imagine what's possible for your organization and set clear, achievable marketing goals to help you get there. I'll also show you strategic ways to gather critical information about your organization and the marketplace. With it, you can begin to make calculated marketing decisions and create a solid foundation for future success.

Principle 2. Story: Connect With the People Who Matter the Most

The second key to being successful with your marketing is all about storytelling. Through real-world case studies and interviews, you'll learn new ways to ensure you're putting your best brand story forward. I'll start by showing you how to build a brand from the ground up or tweak the one you've already got. Then, you'll identify your best assets and spend some time identifying your ideal customers and the people your product or service benefits the most. Finally, you'll put everything together so you tell the right story at the right time, in the right way, to the right people.

Principle 3. Strength: Boost Your Efforts by Extending Your Reach

Collaboration is the name of the game in this third section of the book. You'll have a far better chance of getting results if you team up to tackle your marketing activities. I'll show you interesting ways to do more with your customers and create powerful alliances with individuals and organizations. I'll also show you how to work with the media and other influencers who can help extend your reach and strengthen your efforts. I'll explain why you don't have to do everything on your own and how your marketing can be made much stronger by building a virtual team and working together.

Principle 4. Simplicity: Keep the Plan and Process Straightforward

When it comes right down to it, marketing isn't that complicated. But one of the biggest mistakes I see people make is turning a great idea into a complex plan. They end up over-thinking every step and creating a convoluted process that can take months to implement. In Part IV, I'll show you how to streamline your planning and share ways to make your marketing as effortless and uncomplicated as possible. I'll include some tips and tools to keep you productive and focused on reaching your goals.

You'll also learn how to take advantage of resources right at your fingertips.

Principle 5. Speed: Accelerate and Move Forward

Marketing doesn't need to be time-intensive. There are plenty of things you can do in the short-term—in fact, probably right this minute—to start making a positive impact. In Part V, I'll help you shift gears from planning and show you how to turn your ideas into action that gets real results. Here, you'll put together the final pieces of the puzzle to get immediate performance from your marketing. You'll also learn how to measure your progress along the way and evaluate your results. From there, you can make any necessary course corrections, ensuring your marketing is as successful as possible.

FINAL NOTES

I use these five principles as the core framework or main backbone of the book. You'll see that within each principle's section are related chapters to help you turn the concept into marketing action that works for you and moves you forward. Regardless of your knowledge about marketing, years spent in the work world, or time in academia pursuing an advanced business degree, this streamlined approach will help you get results. It doesn't matter if you're focused on social media or traditional marketing techniques; by using these principles consistently, you'll quickly build market share, boost brand loyalty, and generate more revenue.

The flow of the book is loosely based on a traditional business plan with a twist: All of the sections are modular. The topics and tools are designed to work together in any order to help you quickly create effective and integrated marketing programs that work. If you're more of a linear thinker and prefer to move from one chapter to the next, in a chronological or what's-the-logical-next-step manner, do it. If you're eager to get your name in the news and need to focus on media relations right now, jump ahead to Chapter 7. Slice and dice the content in any way to meet your needs; it's your book, after all.

In this day and age, marketing never stops. People might be talking—or tweeting—about your business right now. That's why I designed this book to be easy to read, absorb, and apply. Many of the tools and techniques here can be implemented in an hour or less. To help you make the most of your time, at the end of every chapter you'll find a Marketing Mindset"section. It includes activities to help you quickly take your organization's pulse and gauge where you are with your marketing. The short quizzes are only five questions long, and every Marketing Mindset is designed to help you immediately apply what you've read and capture your ideas while they're top-of-mind.

I learn best through examples, so I've worked hard to find case studies and real-world stories you'll find both interesting and valuable. I did a significant amount of research and conducted interviews with people from around the world. The results are peppered throughout each chapter as executives, entrepreneurs, and industry leaders share tips and stories. Every example was carefully chosen to help you see how these people apply the core marketing principles in the book and use them to get results for their organizations.

I also want to clarify that I've tried to make the information in this book relevant to a broad range of people. The stories I've included and processes I'm proposing are designed to apply to a CEO of a startup, director of a nonprofit, corporate business manager, marketing student, small business owner, freelance artist, and everyone in between. As a result, throughout the book, you'll see that I use the words *business*, *corporation*, and *organization* interchangeably. I hope you'll replace the words I use with whatever description makes the most sense for you. This goes for *clients*, *customers*, *supporters*, and *members*, too.

Speaking of words, there's one final note I wanted to mention about the following phrases I use in nearly every chapter: *moving forward*, *getting to the next level*, *reaching success*, and *getting the right results*. I've intentionally used these expressions, even though they are somewhat vague, to refer to the results you can achieve through effective marketing. There's a good chance everyone reading this book will have a completely different organizational goal they are trying to reach. It could be getting 1,000 people to like you on Facebook or raising $1 million in revenue. Unfortunately I don't know what you're specifically trying to accomplish with your marketing. I do know that having clear, organizational goals is critical to your success. That's why I'll help you define them upfront in Chapter 1 and then show you how to use your marketing to "move forward," "get to the next level," "get the right results," and "reach success," however you define it.

My ultimate reason for writing *Propel* is to help you rethink your assumptions about marketing. It doesn't have to be complicated, or expensive, or time-consuming. Any activity grounded in strategy, story, strength, simplicity, and speed is powerful. When done right, it will get the right results for your organization. Marketing has the potential to not only benefit your bottom line and bring a lifetime of loyalty from your customers, but also build a rewarding business for you. There's a whole new way to amp up marketing. Let's get started.

PART I

STRATEGY:
Set Your Course for Success

It's incredibly easy to get caught up in an activity trap, in the business of life, to work harder and harder at climbing the ladder of success only to discover it's leaning against the wrong wall.
—Stephen R. Covey

Envisioning your success and setting clear goals to help you get there are the first steps toward effective marketing. The process of defining your goals includes familiarizing yourself with the environment you're working in, including the ins and outs of your business and beyond. Ignoring these initial steps is like trying to build a house without knowing the first thing about construction. Most marketing plans that don't work are short-sighted and lack specific objectives. Others are well-thought-out but performed at the wrong time or in the wrong environment.

In this first section of the book, I'll show you how to be much more calculated and deliberate about your marketing. Using a strategic approach helps you map out a path for success and set solid goals within the context of your business marketplace.

Chapter 1 will help you envision what you need to achieve and identify how to get there. Next, you'll narrow your range of ideas to a manageable level while learning how to avoid the most common pitfalls of goal-setting.

In Chapter 2, you'll learn the importance of defining your landscape, or your business's current situation. You'll take a close look at your business, the competitive environment, and your industry as a whole. This will allow you to identify both challenges and opportunities, further narrowing the scope of your marketing so it's much more effective.

Picking the right priorities up front and getting an accurate lay of the land will help you build a solid foundation before you start rolling up your sleeves and diving into your marketing. Being strategic helps to ensure that you stay focused on the goals that matter the most and find the most powerful position from which to ultimately move your business forward.

CHAPTER 1

Pick Your Priorities

Tamika Vinson works as a financial service counselor helping students navigate the system so they can secure enough money to pursue their educational dreams. But Tamika has a dream of her own. In the next year, she plans to open a retail store for women called iChelle. She's not alone. According to a 2011 report released by Dun & Bradstreet on the state of small business, the United States has seen the highest percentage of start-ups in more than a decade, despite the recession.[1] Tamika's already starting to think about how best to get the word out about her business to potential customers, but she knows before she heads too far down the promotional path she needs to map out a longer-term vision for her business. And she's right.

As I mentioned earlier in the book, marketing is a lot of fun. You get to do all sorts of creative things such as produce videos and hold online contests for your customers. Yet this is part of the reason why so many business owners struggle with marketing. They haven't pictured where they want to go and what they need to do to succeed. They often end up wasting time and resources on ineffective marketing activities and don't get the results they desperately need.

I promise you'll get to focus on all sorts of fun marketing activities very soon, but for now, I don't want you to think about anything specific. I want you to open yourself up to amazing possibilities. To envision your broad future, imagine the big picture of what you're really trying to accomplish and where you ultimately want to be with your business. Believe it or not, in order to be strategic with your marketing, you actually have to do some dreaming first. I'd like you to start thinking about your pie-in-the-sky ideas and extremely lofty ambitions. What I'm describing is your vision.

Many people use the terms *vision* and *mission* interchangeably. However, they are meant to be two entirely different things intended to help you get both inspired and focused. Vision and mission statements are foundational parts of business planning and play a key role in making your marketing work, too. In a nutshell, the vision is a descriptive picture of the future, and the mission is an action statement for the here and now that moves you toward the vision. I'll spend a bit more time on both so you can see the role they play in your business and marketing efforts.

VISION

A vision is intended to be a statement that sums up your organization's aspirations, hopes, and dreams. This phrase describes how your organization envisions the future and what your image is of a perfect world. It's a long-term view of what you're striving for. Most business planning is for a one- to five-year time frame, but an effective vision statement can include a much longer time frame. It's what you envision might be possible in the next 10, 20, maybe even 100 years from now. In fact, you may never achieve it. That's not the point. It's more of a dream; an inspirational message. It gives you a place in the distant horizon to focus on; it's absolutely within sight, but not within reach—yet. It should help motivate you, your staff, and, if you choose to share it externally, even your customers. Change the world. Make things better for kids. Help the environment. These are the things dreams—and vision statements—are made of.

I first came across this type of vision statement back when I worked at Microsoft. At that time, Bill Gates mapped out a very clear vision for the company: Put a computer on every desktop.

This simple, clear statement served a very strategic purpose in exciting customers around the world. It also helped to motivate employees like me. Everyone knew what the company was working toward. Would we ever see it happen? At that time in the industry, it was a huge stretch. But the idea kept us focused and we worked hard to try to get there someday.

Vision statements aren't set in stone. They need to be designed to change and evolve. In time, with the introduction of products such as the Xbox and Internet Explorer, Microsoft was becoming more than just a business putting software CDs in boxes. And as more and more people started to work remotely and on mobile devices, the company needed a new vision statement to re-inspire employees and get customers and partners jazzed again. Microsoft eventually changed its vision: *To help people and businesses throughout the world realize their full potential.* The new sweeping phrase allowed the company to think even more broadly about how it could help people and organizations do more. This vision is still used by the company today.

Here are a few more examples of vision statements:

➡ Nike: "To bring inspiration and innovation to every athlete in the world"

➡ Goodwill Industries International: "To ensure every person has the opportunity to achieve his/her fullest potential and participate in and contribute to all aspects of life"

Keep in mind, the vision for your organization is meant to motivate future action and is not limited by your current situation. In the book *First Things First*, Stephen Covey describes it this way: "...vision is the ability to see beyond our present reality, to create, to invent what does not yet exist, to become what we not yet are. It gives us capacity to live out of our imagination instead of our memory."[2] Here's an example of how to put this into play for a smaller organization. Tamika, the soon-to-be entrepreneur I mentioned at the start of this chapter, also has a vision for her business, iChelle: "To create a nationally recognized brand that helps shape future leaders and uplift neighborhoods."

Fueled by this powerful vision of where she wants to take her business and the positive impact it will make in communities around the United States, Tamika is ready to map out the next strategic part of her planning: her mission statement.

MISSION

If you think of your vision statement as being aspirational, the mission is all about action. In this way, the mission statement works hand-in-hand with the vision. It touches on the core purpose of your organization and what you're doing now to strive toward reaching your vision in the future. What steps are you taking to bring that vision closer and within reach?

To give you an example of how the two statements work together, here's an inspirational vision statement for Dress for Success, an international nonprofit organization dedicated to improving the lives of women in 110 cities across 12 countries. The organization provides professional clothing, employment retention programs, and ongoing support to its clients, helping them be self-sufficient and professionally successful. Its vision is: "To promote the economic independence of disadvantaged women."

Now take a look at the organization's mission statement. It does a good job of explaining how Dress for Success plans to take action and work toward making that vision come true: "We help disadvantaged women find and maintain employment, become financially savvy, improve their health and wellness, and achieve self-defined success."

Now I want to shift gears and focus again on Tamika's business. She too has a mission statement that is intended to help her take the right steps today to reach her longer-term vision for iChelle: "To help women feel confident, comfortable, and beautiful by providing affordable, upscale fashion and career development opportunities."

Do you see how this message supports Tamika's long-term vision for the business? She eventually plans to grow iChelle by adding new locations and potentially franchising once the company's brand is nationally recognized. She also plans to give back to the community by creating jobs and internship opportunities. She's unable to do all of these things in the first few years of her business, but she's now on a mission to work toward reaching them.

VALUES

For an organization's vision and mission to truly be effective, they must both reflect the organization's values. These are the core beliefs in your business that are shared with everyone internally and, in many cases, externally. They help define and determine your culture and work together with your vision and mission. The three form a helpful framework you can use to better run your business and make smarter, more strategic marketing decisions.

On a personal level, our values come into play on a daily basis. If you value having a healthy lifestyle, you probably demonstrate that value by watching what you eat and exercising regularly. You may make a decision to invest in a gym membership or take time to go on a long walk with a friend a few times a week.

Business values are no different. They are usually a list of words or statements that outline what's important to your organization and the core things that will guide and influence your attitudes and behavior. For example, if your organization values professional development, you might support an employee who wants to help your marketing efforts by speaking on an expert panel for the chamber of commerce. If you value work-life balance, you can justify your decision to leave work early on Thursday to attend an after-hours wine-tasting to have fun discovering new bottles. And who knows, you just might end up doing some networking and exploring new business development opportunities as well.

With more than 310 stores in North America and the United Kingdom, Whole Foods is a global leader in the natural and organic food business.[3] The company has done an excellent job of creating a set of core values that accurately reflect what is truly important to the organization. They not only support the organization's vision and mission of environmental sustainability and corporate responsibility, but they are also the underpinning of the company's culture and are intended to remain constant. Whole Foods's Website reads, "Many people feel Whole Foods Market is an exciting company of which to be a part and a very special place to work. These core values are the primary reasons for this feeling, and they transcend our size and our growth rate. By maintaining these core values, regardless of how large a company Whole Foods Market becomes, we can preserve what has always been special about our company. These core values are the soul of our company:

➠ Selling the highest quality natural and organic products available

➠ Satisfying and delighting our customers

➠ Supporting team member happiness and excellence

➠ Creating wealth through profits and growth

➠ Caring about our communities and our environment

➠ Creating ongoing win-win partnerships with our suppliers

➠ Promoting the health of our stakeholders through healthy eating education."

Do you see how these values statements would then help Whole Foods make smarter, more strategic decisions about its marketing? For example, on the company's blog, it features a two-minute video about Gaia Herbs, a certified organic herb farm in the Blue Ridge Mountains of western North Carolina. Located on 250 acres of certified organic river bottom soil and growing roughly 50 different crops, the farm is one of the largest medicinal herb farms in the United States.[4] This directly supports many of Whole Foods's values, including selling the highest quality of organic products, creating partnerships with suppliers, and delighting customers.

Tamika is still working to finalize her list of company values, but she knows they will include the following principles she thinks are important, not only to the success of iChelle, but also to the satisfaction of her customers:

➠ Offering high-quality products

➠ Delivering exceptional service

➠ Providing support and career development for staff

➠ Creating an inviting experience in-store and online

➠ Improving our local communities

GOALS

Once you've got your vision, mission, and values mapped out, the next things you need to clarify are your goals and objectives. They too help serve as a compass to keep you pointed in the right direction. If you find yourself in a new environment or situation and you get off track, you can refer back to them to become realigned. With a clear goal in hand, even if you wander off the trail a bit to check out a squirrel (or explore a new social media tool), you can easily get right back to focusing on where you need to go.

Here we again have two terms that can be easily confused with each other—*goals* and *objectives*. I'll start with goals. You can think of them as slightly more defined versions of your vision statement. Goals come in all shapes and sizes. There are long-term goals and short-term goals, big ones and little ones, easy-to-do goals and very challenging ones. It doesn't matter where you start; you just need to pick one. For example, on a personal level, your goal might be to take a trip to Europe, learn how to cook a soufflé, or start getting massages more often. Now let's shift gears and put the practice of goal-setting into business terms.

Here is a list of common goals that you might want to accomplish:

➠ Earn more revenue.

➠ Secure more customers.

➠ Hold an event.

➠ Open a second location.

➠ Produce Web videos.

➠ Get your name in the news.

➠ Get more hits to your Website.

Tamika's business hasn't launched yet, but she's already defined one clear goal: Successfully open iChelle's first location.

Do you see how all of these goals are somewhat vague? They make sense but, because they are broad, there is still plenty of room for more specific details. That's where your objectives come into play.

OBJECTIVES

The term *objective* is used all the time in marketing, even though it has a stiff, formal, military tone. In fact, if you look up the word, you'll often see that the first definition listed is related to its use in the military: "A military objective is a clearly defined desired result in a given campaign, major operation, battle, or engagement set by the senior command for their formations and units to achieve."[5] This is no surprise, as many researchers say the first real marketing began after World War II, when governments used

PR and marketing as propaganda and as promotional tools for their education and health programs.

Whether you're in the military or not, objectives help take your goals to the next level and put something in place to help you measure the effectiveness of your marketing. If you give your goal a little more meat so it's clear, measurable, and has a due date, you can better evaluate your results. Here's my simple definition of an objective: what you're specifically going to do to reach your goal by a deadline.

For example, you can set a fitness goal of "getting in shape," but it will be hard to gauge your results on the scale or in inches—and know when to do the actual measuring—if you don't add some clarifying details. You'll be much more successful in reaching that goal if you say something along the lines of, "I want to lose 10 pounds and go down at least one clothing size in the next three months, starting tomorrow." See what I mean? Now *that's* something you can get your arms around, start working toward, and measure—literally.

SMART OBJECTIVES

A well-known tool a lot of people use to help them convert a broad goal into a more defined action step is called a SMART objective. *SMART* is an acronym that George T. Doran developed in the 1980s.[6] He was the former director of corporate planning for Washington Water Power Company in Spokane, Washington, and came up with the acronym to help people remember the criteria that go into a crystal-clear objective:

Specific: Be sure your objective is as precise and detailed as possible, and details exactly what needs to get done.

Measurable: Come up with a quantifiable number tied to what you need to do so you can determine if you made progress or not.

Assignable: Make sure you assign a name and owner to the task so you know who, if not you, is going to get the work done.

Realistic: Do you have the time, money, and other resources needed to get the task accomplished?

Time-related: Give yourself a deadline for when the project needs to be completed.

To better understand how you can convert a goal into a SMART objective, I want you to refer back to Tamika's goal of successfully opening iChelle's first location. This sounds great, but how does she take the first step toward making it happen? Should she start by building a potential customer mailing list? Create a Facebook page? Let her local media outlets and bloggers know the store is about to open?

Instead of trying to guess what to do next, Tamika took time up front to outline several SMART objectives for her company. This ensures that her marketing will be much more strategic and effective in moving her business forward in the direction she needs it to go.

Here are a few examples of some of her SMART objectives:

➡ Secure a retail space under 4,000 square feet located in The Landing shopping mall in Renton, Washington, by June of 2013.

➡ Ensure that 50 percent of all first-time shoppers return within three months of their initial visit.

Are they specific? Yes. Measureable? I think so. Assignable? Right now they are all on her to-do list, but once she begins to generate revenue, she can consider delegating some of the work to her staff or even hire a marketing consultant, especially to meet the objective of getting that first round of shoppers back in iChelle's doors. Tamika says the objectives are realistic, based on her expertise and available time and resources. And speaking of time, both objectives have clear, measureable deadlines.

GOALS AND OBJECTIVES WORK TOGETHER

Hopefully you see how a SMART objective builds upon the original goal and makes it much more specific. Now you can really roll up your sleeves and get to work. You have some idea of how you'll evaluate your progress to see if you meet—or even exceed—that initial goal. Your goal and objective work together to help you design and define your desired result. They translate your initial vision and mission statements into concrete ideas and clear steps to start making things happen.

Here's another example of how the power of strategic thinking, and how goals and objectives work together for you. There's a great coffee shop where I like to work called Zoka. They sell a variety of caffeinated drinks, yummy pastries, and sandwiches. Assume for a minute they hit a slow period for a few weeks and don't sell as many food items as usual. They end up having to toss an increasing number of leftover perishable goodies at closing time.

Zoka could set a simple goal: Start selling more pastries. Then, to give that goal more direction, the owner might create a supporting SMART objective like this: "All evening baristas will sell 50 percent more dessert pastries in the next week." A strategic goal and objective like this adds tremendous benefit to the business and its staff. The employees have a clear understanding of what they need to work toward and what their sales responsibilities are by the end of each shift. The manager is also aware of what needs to be accomplished and can measure the results to see if the team is on track, and could even consider giving an incentive to the barista who sells the most.

THE DIFFERENCE BETWEEN A DREAM AND A GOAL

Some people don't see the difference between a dream and a goal. As I mentioned earlier, a dream is more about your vision, or what *could be* for your organization. You may never actually accomplish it, and hopefully I've shown you by now that your chances are especially slim without a clear goal and SMART objective. Here's an example from a personal perspective: A dream might be something such as, "I want to travel abroad someday." If you want to really pursue this dream, you would take it to the next level and turn it into a supporting goal along the lines of "I will travel to Europe in the next two years." And then from there, if you really want to see that original dream come to life, you would get even more specific and come up with a SMART objective for yourself: "I will save $3,000 to travel to Spain for a week in April of 2015."

CREATIVE PEOPLE NEED GOALS, TOO

If you're a writer, artist, or another creative type, I know that the process of setting goals can sometimes feel as though it will stifle your innovative ideas. But this doesn't have to be the case. Thinking about your long-term vision and what you need to do to get there can help you break out of the starving-artist mode and better channel your creative energy and valuable time. One of the best examples I know of someone who lives by this process is Brett Renville, a successful cinematographer and fashion photographer. His long-term vision is to have one of his photos on the cover of *Vogue* and a documentary accepted into the Sundance Film Festival. To get there someday, he's working on being more strategic and choosing projects that will grow his business in the direction he wants to go. By making his goal-setting a deliberate part of his business, he stays focused on the task, meets his clients' needs, and still has time left over to spend in his organic garden and cook vegan meals with his girlfriend.

An example of one of his recent projects was an opportunity to fly to Rwanda by the non-governmental organization (NGO), Kageno. The organization hired him to document its humanitarian efforts in Banda Village, a rural African village only accessible by a four-hour bus ride and a two-hour trek into the jungle's rain forest. Brett's goal was to capture some compelling footage, and his SMART objective was to complete nine, three-minutes videos by May 2012. Before committing, he needed to think through every aspect of the project and his overall work schedule to be sure he could meet the needs of his client and also meet the deadline. As a solo entrepreneur, he has to be realistic about what he can accomplish, as there is only so much time in the day. As a result of this project in Rwanda, Brett will have one of his videos shown at a major fundraising event in Los Angeles in the next year. In addition to the film being used to further the humanitarian efforts by Kageno, this project is also moving Brett one step closer to his dreams.

COMMONLY ASKED QUESTIONS

A question I am often asked is, Can you have more than one goal and objective? Yes, of course! You can and should have as many as you need to stay focused on what needs to get done, by whom, and by when. Just keep the list manageable. Remember, part of a SMART objective is making sure that what you do is realistic according to your available time, resources, staffing, and so on.

Another question that's often raised is about the difference between business and marketing goals. Sometimes it's helpful to have both, and you'll see this a lot in larger organizations. The vision, mission, and values don't change, and the process of determining goals is the same, but business goals always come first. Once they're set and you look at what needs to get done, only then do you create marketing goals to support the direction you need to go in. Business goals should drive your marketing activities, not vice versa.

One way to think of this is similar to that video most of the airlines show before takeoff, in which the adult puts on her own oxygen mask before putting a mask on the child in the next seat: You need to make sure your business goals are taken care of before you start creating marketing plans. I've seen many companies make marketing mistakes because of this. They were busy, busy, busy doing marketing activities, but not getting any results that actually boosted the business's bottom line. You might make a big splash with a social media campaign or cool direct mail piece, but if it has nothing to do with your goal of driving traffic to your Website, it won't ultimately move you in the right direction. You want more than one spike in your sales. You want a steady flow that carries you forward.

For example, a financial services business might set a business goal of generating more revenue. A supporting marketing goal might be to create a customer appreciation program. Both are vague, but the second one, the marketing goal, is a bit more specific about the promotional activity to be used. Then you need to get even more specific from there by defining a SMART marketing objective. For example, the objective could be: "The sales team will hold an exclusive monthly lunch for 50 VIP customers for three months, starting June 15, to renew full contracts with 75 percent of customers by December 31." In this way, you're clarifying your marketing activity and ensuring it not only meets your marketing goal, but also supports your higher-level business goal.

PROACTIVE VS. REACTIVE

Part of the reason why goal planning is so important is that it forces you to slow down a bit and think through your priorities. It gives you time to dream of the future, picture where you want to be, and map out what you need to accomplish to get there. This is easier said than done, especially in our fast-paced culture in which we live in the moment and all of those phone calls, e-mails, texts, and meetings have to be tended to now, now, now! But I promise you, if you slow down just a bit, define your vision and mission, and set goals with clear objectives, you will see results from your marketing activities.

Tamika is already starting to see this happen with her business. She's thinking through sales scenarios with her customers, as well as generating marketing ideas—both important steps toward launching her business in the coming year. By taking time to envision what success looks like, she's already got the start of a strategic business plan.

The other benefit of being proactive and strategic with your planning is that you'll be better prepared when a real crisis hits and you need to react. Too often in marketing, we think we're at our best when we fly by the seat of our pants, reacting to every new opportunity and situation that crops up. We tell ourselves we're good at going with our gut, and that it means we're on top of our game. But this isn't always the case. Improvisation has its place, but delivering a well-rehearsed performance is equally impressive.

TIMING

There are certain times of the year when most of us are focused on goal setting. January is an obvious time when everyone is thinking about New Year's resolutions and kicking off business planning. Some corporations are on a fiscal calendar and do their planning mid-year. There is no wrong or right season. Just set your goals as soon as possible and stay on top of what you're doing to reach them.

USING A SCORECARD

A helpful strategic planning method I've encountered throughout the years, which most large corporations use to move their organizations forward, is using a scorecard tool. This lets you integrate the goals and SMART objectives you've defined with your strategy. The simple grid I'm providing here is adapted from work done by Dr. Robert Kaplan (Harvard Business School) and Dr. David Norton on the Balanced Scorecard, and it's beneficial for micro-entrepreneurs as well as to Fortune 500 corporations.[7]

CHAPTER 2

Map the Landscape

In order to be more strategic with your marketing, it's crucial to have a broad perspective on your business, inside and out. Think of it as looking at your organization through bifocal lenses: Beyond just using the distance lens to focus on the vision for your organization, you also need to use the up-close lens to get a clear sense of what's going on directly in front of you, especially when it comes to your employees, customer base, and marketing activities. You'll round out your perspective and be more effective if you keep an eye on both internal and external elements impacting your business.

In some cases, you need to literally get out of your business and observe what's happening in the world around you. If you have a Web-based business, that means letting go of the mouse, keeping your phone in your pocket, and observing your business from the other side of the keyboard now and then. Without this bird's-eye perspective, you may never fully see all of the opportunities within your reach. The more information you have about your current situation and the environment you're working in, the more you can use it to your advantage and help your business reach its marketing potential.

One of the best ways to gather the information you need is to perform what's called a situational analysis. It's a helpful three-step process that gives you a great snapshot of where you are and what's happening around you. It helps you identify what's working and pinpoint what isn't. First, you observe what's going on in and around your business and capture all of the facts. Second, you analyze all of the information you've discovered. The third step is to dig deeper, if necessary, and gather any important details you're missing. After completing these three steps, you are in a good position to make some smart strategic decisions about your best assets so you can leverage them throughout your marketing efforts.

The purpose of doing a situational analysis is to provide you with a quick snapshot of what you have to work with and the contextual setting. It forces you to consider the entire landscape in and around your organization. This includes the good and the great, as well as the bad and the ugly. As I've mentioned before, when it comes to marketing, some people tend to focus on what they think they need to do before they have the data to back up their ideas. They think, for example, "I need to send a press release! Let's hold an event!" But sometimes they miss the best opportunities right under their noses that could strategically help move them forward.

This process doesn't have to be complicated. You're just compiling what I call a quick-n-dirty brain dump. I had the pleasure of facilitating a situational analysis exercise for a group of hard-working entrepreneurs in the hospitality industry. They were all part of the Seattle Bed and Breakfast (B&B) Association and needed help determining how to best use their marketing efforts to educate the public about the benefits of staying in B&Bs. There were roughly 10 people around a table and, in a little more than an hour, I guided them through the three steps, which I am about to share with you.

STEP 1. CAPTURE THE FACTS

To ensure the process went smoothly, I introduced the group to a tool called a SWOT grid to help guide the discussion and loosely structure their thinking. A management consultant named Albert Humphrey came up with the SWOT technique back in the 1960s. *SWOT* is an acronym for *strengths*, *weaknesses*, *opportunities*, and *threats*.[1] The strengths and weaknesses categories are intended to help you identify elements within your organization. The other two, opportunities and threats, are related to external factors that impact your organization.

INTERNAL	Strengths	Weaknesses
EXTERNAL	Opportunities	Threats

Once you're ready to begin, you simply start taking an inventory of your current situation, conducting an informal review of your company from the inside out, starting with all of your business's advantages and disadvantages. These can range from the limited number of employees you have to your impressive list of customer testimonials. If you're a solo business owner, you would also focus on *you* and *your personal* strengths and weaknesses. They might include anything from your many years of professional experience to a lack of technical knowledge, depending on what you determine as adding value or holding back your success.

Some people prefer to start with the negative by identifying all of the challenges they're facing. That's a perfectly fine way to begin, by listing everything that's going wrong. You can think of it as a venting or therapy session for your business. To get going, you might ask yourself, "What marketing issues keep me up at night? What are my greatest concerns about the competition? What trends do I think I'm behind on in my industry?" Isolate every weakness you think you have and get all of the concerning information out of your head and onto paper or a laptop where you can look at it objectively.

Another approach to this process is to do the complete opposite and start things off on a positive note: Identify all of your all strengths and opportunities. If you're an optimist like me, you'll easily be able to come up with a long list. What awards and recognition have you received? What makes your products and services far better or different from those of your competitors? What's going well with your marketing? What good relationships do you have with customers? Do you have any noteworthy alliances with other organizations? Here, your eyes are only on the good elements—your opportunities, strengths, and greatest assets.

It doesn't matter which approach you take, whether starting with the challenges or kicking off on the high notes, just pick one and make sure you discuss both sides of the spectrum. Keep in mind this process is like a brainstorming session; you're gathering existing facts and data, as well as capturing any new ideas that crop up. Gather as much information as you can right now, getting the lay of the land and identifying facts about what's working and what's not. It works best if you hold off on analyzing or critiquing anything at this point.

As you work your way through this process, you'll move from the inside of your business out to the broadest edge of your industry. First, you focus on your company, and you start listing everything that's going on, both good and bad. What's the situation when it comes to your employees, your customers, your pricing, and everything else you can think of? And don't forget to include your marketing! In some ways, you're creating an enhanced pros-and-cons list. It's that simple.

Then you shift gears and examine all of the external factors impacting your business; things such as the competition and your industry. You look for opportunities as well as possible threats—anything you need to be aware of and keep top of mind. Two things to examine are your potential partners and direct and indirect competitors. If you're a nonprofit that helps feed the homeless, what other organizations in your area are offering similar services? Who else vies for your customer's time, money, and mindshare? What are they doing that's better than what you're doing, and where do you stand above the pack? Are there any opportunities to partner with other organizations and businesses?

Another element to review is your industry itself. What is going on in your marketplace? What are the big external issues impacting your organization? Is the media focused on certain hot issues right now? What are they? What are your customers talking about or concerned about? These are often things that are out of your control and might be dictated by things such as government regulations or even pop culture. I should note here that some business owners, when asked about their industry, have no idea what the current trends are or who the competitors are in their market. In some cases, when asked specifically about their competition, they'll go as far as to say their product or service is so unique, they don't have any threats. Although it would be great if that were true, it's not; every organization has some level of competition. You've got to have a realistic picture of the environment you're doing business in if you're going to be successful in navigating the lay of the land.

These are the main categories I use when I'm conducting a SWOT analysis with organizations, but you can certainly add more. For example, you could break your company's strengths and weaknesses down even further to examine the pros and cons of things like your employee training process, customer relationships, product pricing, and so on. Just remember to keep it strategic and focus on the most important elements impacting your internal and external environment.

The Seattle Bed & Breakfast Association

Here's exactly how the B&B group worked through the SWOT grid and started to use it to put their marketing in motion. They began by discussing the strengths and weaknesses for each of their individual businesses. They quickly realized that, whereas they all offered common amenities such as free Wi-Fi and complimentary breakfasts, they had a tremendous number of unique assets. For example, the Three Tree Point B&B provided guests with spectacular views overlooking Puget Sound and Mount Rainier. The Shafer Baillie Mansion boasted a magnificent, 14,000-square-foot Tudor Revival home and was just a block from Seattle's Volunteer Park, with its botanical garden and conservatory, as well as the Seattle Asian Art Museum. A third, the Green Lake Guest House, served gourmet, made-to-order entrees such as swedish pancakes and brie, and apple-stuffed French toast garnished with seasonal herbs and edible flowers directly from its garden. The group clearly had a wide range of unique offerings, but they had their challenges, too. Despite all of these terrific amenities and services, they weren't getting enough year-round business or booking to capacity.

Then, the B&B group shifted the conversation and began reviewing the strengths and weaknesses of their association as a whole. One thing the

rooms and apartments were not regulated. One unhappy guest described the site in this way: "For what's supposed to be an ultra-hyped, sexy start-up, Airbnb seems like a dressed-up version of Craigslist, and not in a good way."[3] Unlike Airbnb, all of the Seattle B&B group's properties are fully licensed and inspected. That's an important and valuable difference to many potential customers and it plays directly to an advantage of the B&B group. This noteworthy fact was something they could use strategically by highlighting it in their marketing activities and promoting it to the media and other opinion influencers.

STEP 3. DIG DEEPER

Throughout this process, you're discovering as many nuggets of helpful information as possible. Eventually you'll start to see the bits of marketing gold emerge from this situational snapshot. When you've scratched the surface and found something with potential, you need to dig deeper to gather even more specific data. For example, a hypnotherapist I worked with specialized in helping child athletes reach their goals. This strength of his had tremendous marketing potential, but he needed to do additional research to get actual statistics on his success rates before he could use this in his messaging. Another business I worked with, a jewelry designer, realized the majority of her clients were actually men, not women. These customers were buying her high-end pieces as special occasion gifts for the women they loved. In order to better promote her new jewelry line to those men, she needed to do additional research to learn more about them to ensure her marketing activities resonated with them.

This is exactly what happened during the SWOT session with the Seattle Bed & Breakfast group. They realized some of their greatest word-of-mouth marketing opportunities were just a few blocks away: their neighbors. I was one of those people. Until I met with the group, I wasn't aware my condo was within a mile of three historic B&Bs. The next time my family decided to visit me at the same time and I was unable to put everyone up in my little guest room, I was now better educated about the value of B&Bs. Without hesitation, I would suggest they stay there or, even better, offer to pay for it as a treat. So cultivating relationships with people like me, a B&B neighbor, could be a strategic marketing move. But before the group launched into a full-blown campaign covering the doorknobs of all of the neighboring houses with promotional fliers, they needed to dig deeper. I advised them to do some research about how likely neighbors are to refer friends and family and possibly host a series of low-cost open houses just for homeowners within walking distance to give them a peek inside and help educate them about the benefits of B&Bs.

Extra Research

Just about any information you happen to need can usually be found in a few clicks on Google or Bing. But there are many more methods to consider using when you need to pinpoint specific data. If you determine you do need to perform more research, it's helpful to know what kind of data you need before you get started. Research tends to fall into two categories: quantitative or qualitative.

Quantitative research, as the name implies, counts things. It examines how many customers came to your store last week, or how many people checked "agree strongly" on a survey asking if your Website is easy to use. These are mathematical measurements, usually done with large, group samples in a controlled manner with tools such as questionnaires and surveys.

Qualitative research, on the other hand, deals with matters not easily counted, such as how a customer feels while in your store or how customers initially found your Website. This research helps you gather information about your customers' behavior, decision-making processes, and reasoning. It is usually done in smaller, concentrated samples of your customers through interviews, focus groups, and actual observations of participants interacting with your product or service.

Here are examples of both types of research that the B&B group discussed:

➠ **Quantitative:** How likely are you to refer a family member to a bed and breakfast within six blocks of your home? Circle one: Very Likely, Likely, Unlikely.

➠ **Qualitative:** What amenities are most important to you when considering referring a friend or family member to stay in a nearby bed and breakfast?

Once you know what additional information you need, then you've got to determine the best way to get it. There are several methods for accessing existing research or conducting your own. *Primary research* refers to research you've done that you can draw upon, such as past feedback on surveys. *Secondary research* refers to reviewing and using external research. This might come in the form of a report you read in a trade publication or a "research shows 9 out of 10 people prefer it" article you read in an online media outlet.

With any research, whether it's primary or secondary, it's important to be aware of variables that can influence the results of the study. You'll want to keep these things in mind:

➠ **Geographic:** Location that could impact thoughts and behaviors

➠ **Demographic:** Age, gender, education traits that shape attitude and behavior

➠ **Psychographic:** Personality traits that drive behavior

➠ **Behavioristic:** Values and experiences that impact opinions and behaviors

If you decide you need to conduct your own primary research, there are a lot of different tools and techniques to consider. Here are a few of my personal favorites that don't require a lot of time, money, or other resources, and always deliver powerful insights and tremendous value to all organizations.

Focus Groups

I can't say enough good things about focus groups. I've participated in many of them, ranging from movie reviews to chili taste tests. I've also helped conduct a slew of them throughout the years for Microsoft, American Express, small businesses, and other organizations. You gather a number of customers together for the purpose of listening to their honest opinions about your product or service. These groups can be formal: done in a conference room with a facilitator, sometimes recorded and in some cases using a two-way mirror. Other types of focus groups can be done in an informal setting: gathering a handful of customers together over coffee or wine and asking for their feedback. If you provide them with a list of topics to discuss or questions to answer, you can let them do it on their own, asking one participant to facilitate the conversation and another to take notes or record the discussion. Without you in the room, they'll be more likely to share honest opinions. It doesn't matter exactly how you do it, just get a group of people together, give them something to talk about, and, most importantly, listen.

Surveys

Surveys are great as well. Thanks to companies such as surveymonkey.com, anyone can send a simple 10-question e-survey to 100 people—for free. Surveymonkey ensures all responses are anonymous and lets you track every answer and do some basic level of analysis. The secret to an effective survey is to keep your list of questions short and your question types simple; you don't want them to be too long or too complex or people won't make it to the end. You also need to design your questions to provide the right results so you have information you can readily use. A question such as "Do you like our product?" may not give you much insight if everyone answers *yes* or *no*. Making a simple tweak to the question and asking "*Why* do you like our product?" gives you much more valuable answers. I'll talk more about how to quickly assess and use the results of your survey in Chapter 10.

External Sources of Information

As I mentioned earlier, another great way to obtain information, especially about your industry, is to use secondary research available through external sources such as trade or professional organizations. For example, some of the groups I belong to include the American Marketing Association (AMA), the International Association of Business Communicators, the Chamber of Commerce, and the Public Relations Society of America (PRSA). I could contact any of them to ask about market trends, policies impacting my industry, or reports on hot issues—often for no additional fee. For example, when I last checked the AMA's Website, there was an article on how new government regulations and increasing patient knowledge are creating an inhospitable environment for pharmaceutical marketing strategies.

PART II

STORY:

Connect With the People Who Matter Most

In marketing you must choose between boredom, shouting, and seduction. Which do you want?

—Roy H. Williams

With a solid strategy behind your marketing, after you've set some reasonable goals and scanned the marketplace to identify your best opportunities, it's time to think about your story: who you are, what you have to say, and who needs to know. It's time to dig into the facts behind your product or service and figure out the most meaningful way to share them.

In Chapter 3, you'll focus on your brand and learn how to use the unique characteristics of your business to set you apart from your competition. Here, you'll identify your best features and acknowledge the most important facts about your business. When you pull it all together, you'll create meaningful stories that connect with your ideal customers and help your organization shine.

Once you're clear about the power of your brand, the natural next step is to determine the people in the marketplace who need what you're offering—these are the people you'll tell your story to through marketing activities. Who cares about your brand and wants to listen to your story? If your answer is "everyone," you'll need to hone it to increase your chances to move forward effectively. Targeting your story to too large an audience is like playing the lottery: It's nice if you win, but your odds of success are mighty low. It's better to focus on a few, smaller receptive groups and tailor your marketing messages to them.

In Chapter 4, I'll shed some light on how to define your target audience so you can focus your marketing efforts in the right direction. I'll share several real-life cases of businesses that succeeded in transforming a broad marketplace into a specific set of niche opportunities with customers.

Giving your brand the attention it deserves will ensure you have a good story to tell and help you create a distinct place in the market. From there, you can select specific segments of customers who align with your brand and listen to your stories.

CHAPTER 3

Build Your Brand

FOR MORE THAN 20 years, the Gap has used a navy blue box surrounding its three-letter name in a traditional white font as its logo. The logo has played an important part in illustrating the company's brand as the classic one-stop-shop for basic denim. But in time, customer needs changed and new competitors in the apparel industry such as H&M and Forever 21 appeared on the horizon to deliver more hip, fresh styles.[1] At the time of this identity crisis, the Gap's senior management decided it was time for the company to evolve its brand to be more modern, and that included making a change to its classic logo. On the surface, there was nothing wrong with this decision. Other corporations, such as Nike, McDonald's, and Apple, have successfully tweaked their visual look and feel. But the Gap's revamped logo didn't fare so well.

With this design revision, the company's name was now presented in a simple, black, Helvetica font, intersected by a small, faded blue box just to the right of the letter "p." Immediately after the company launched the new logo on its Website, it was hit with thousands of critical comments.[2] Social media channels buzzed with people around the world who were outraged with how the Gap chose to refresh its visual identity, especially among the graphic design and branding communities. The public protest included more than 2,000 comments on Facebook criticizing the decision to ditch the well-known logo, and a Twitter account set up in protest collected nearly 5,000 followers. On top of that, a "Make your own Gap logo" site attracted nearly 14,000 entries and mock versions.[3]

Forced to backpedal on its initial direction, the company ended up dumping the new design just four days after its creation and pushed its original font back into its familiar blue box.[4]

Part of the reason organizations, large and small, struggle with branding is that they equate their brand with a logo. They make the mistake of putting all their branding eggs into the logo basket, investing a great deal of time and money trying to design the perfect icon. But if they don't build meaning beyond that little symbol, it falls flat. A well-designed visual identity can be an important part of your story, but it is just that: one part. There's much more to building a strong brand than creating a logo.

That's why effective brands aren't built overnight. It takes time to develop an authentic, integrated, and memorable experience for your customers. And it's incredibly important to make this investment in your brand. It's a powerful driver for your marketing and crucial to the long-term success of your business. When done right, branding gives you the key to unlocking your customers' hearts, minds, and souls—and in some cases, their credit card. It helps you go beyond yammering to your customers about your products and services to actually connecting with them.

Like it or not, we judge other people in the first few seconds of meeting them. And this goes for businesses as well. Picture a restaurant with a grimy window, dilapidated awning, and overflowing garbage can out front. Are you enticed to have lunch there? Or how about a neon pink Website with bright yellow font and a musical pop-up ad you can't close fast enough? Or a confusing voice mail system that traps you in a series of loops and won't let you press a single button to reach a real person. We make snap decisions all the time about the companies we will—and won't—do business with, and these decisions are directly based on our perception of the organization's brand. In some ways, your brand is like virtual giftwrap: It's the promise of what customers will get if they like what they see and choose to open up the package and do business with you. It enables you to tap into customers' deepest needs and wants—not just intellectually, but also emotionally. You're not just selling a product or service; you're selling a solution.

This is why your brand is so essential. In the Introduction of this book, I touched on how branding is the core of your organization and can even be described as the unique personality of the business. At the center of everything you do, it's a driving force for your overall business. It helps you influence how customers think, feel, and behave in response to your product or service. Branding helps you put everything at your disposal into play and start telling your story.

Imagine your organization is like a bicycle. Picture your brand at the center of both wheels. In this way, it serves as the connecting hub for all of your marketing activities. They extend out from around the brand, like spokes. Interconnected, they work together to create consistent marketing messages that tell the right story. Your brand supports your business and works hard to ensure your marketing is aligned and moving you forward. It is much easier to make decisions about your marketing if you have taken time to define your brand up front.

Soon Beng Yeap is chief marketing officer at Regis University in Denver, Colorado, and is exceptionally wise when it comes to storytelling through branding. He started his career as a journalist with Reuters in London and newspapers in Malaysia, continuing on in senior executive roles as a strategic business and brand advisor for businesses around the world, including Starbucks and Microsoft. He and I had the opportunity to work together when he brought me on board to help conduct a situational analysis of Seattle University's social media programs. He wanted to encourage everyone on campus, from professors to career advisors, to use tools such as Twitter and Facebook, but needed to ensure the university's brand was accurately reflected.

In order to do this, he created a loose set of guidelines to inspire and inform people about using social media on behalf of the university's brand. "You don't try to get your customers to *fall in line*, you try to get them to *fall in love* with your brand," said Soon Beng. By *customers*, he means everyone the university impacted, from students and their parents to alumni and even local restaurants across the street from the school. With this approach to branding, he and his team helped build the university's reputation and share its story. "To achieve brand nirvana, you must be able to stir the soul of your customers," he continued. Today, Seattle University is rated one of the top 10 schools by *US News & World Report*.

But as the Gap logo story demonstrates, all of your hard work can evaporate in a matter of minutes if you don't stay on top of managing your brand. If you've already done your branding work, your organization probably has developed a set of standards to help steer you through any marketing issues that may come your way. With your vision and goals as your compass and your branding guidelines as your map, you can easily navigate designing a Website or creating a brochure that effectively tells your story. If you don't have branding guidelines in place, I'll show you how to build upon the solid marketing foundation you've created so far and layer in another piece: your brand.

Creating an effective brand is a process, and maintaining your image and reputation takes time. And even with planning, your brand continues to develop organically throughout the years and is impacted by many factors, much like a person's identity. But there are some steps you can take now to make the branding journey a little faster, easier, and more manageable. It's important to take time up front to figure out what your brand is and what it stands for, because you'll use your brand to fuel the rest of your marketing.

STEP 1. LIST YOUR BRAND ATTRIBUTES

How do you begin to build your brand? The first step is to identify your unique brand attributes or qualities. You need to develop a short list of words that accurately reflect who you are and what you do. These become the first pieces of your branding guidebook that will work together with other parts of your brand to help tell your story.

Maria Ross is a branding expert I've collaborated with in the past few years. In her book, *Branding Basics for Small Business*, she includes an interesting exercise to demonstrate the power of a brand. In it, you start by picking a well-known company or nonprofit you like. It could be Disney, Neiman Marcus, Apple, or the Girl Scouts; it doesn't matter. The next step is to write down a few words or phrases that come to mind when you think of the organization's characteristics.

Take Neiman Marcus, for example. For more than a century, The Neiman Marcus Group has focused on building an image of a premier luxury retailer. When I use this exercise in my workshops, people have no trouble coming up with a list of words to describe the retail chain, including: *expensive, unique merchandise, upscale, fashion-forward,* and *superior service.* Nearly everyone in the room has at least one of these words on his or her list, and they all agree they accurately describe qualities of the Neiman Marcus brand. This is the power of an effective brand: clear, consistent, and memorable. If a brand is managed well, these words, or "attributes," are reflected in everything the company does, including its Website design, store window displays, giftwrap, staff dress code, store return policies, logo, and so on.

"The brand informs every decision a company makes about marketing and running the company in general," says Maria. "Would Neiman Marcus advertise at a monster truck rally? Would its marketing team hire cheap designers to create their in-store signage? Absolutely not."

To get started creating a list of key words that describe your organization's brand attributes, repeat the exercise I just described—only this time your company is the focus. I encourage you to come up with your own list first, but then branch out and test your results. Ask your employees to come up with a list. Do the words match? Ask your very best clients to list your attributes. Is your image of your company in sync with your customers' perception of your brand? Review testimonials and feedback you've received about your services and products. What key words pop up repeatedly? Are customers describing your brand the way you want them to? The purpose of this exercise is to test your initial thinking and ensure your brand is consistent in the minds of the people who interact with your business the most. If you're an existing business, this is a great way to see if your marketing is communicating a consistent image. And if you're a new business, it will help you uncover potential attributes about your brand you could consider using when you're ready to start marketing.

STEP 2. CREATE YOUR BRAND PACKAGE

The next step is to move beyond just a few words and to try to capture the comprehensive feeling, character, or personality your brand conveys.

Maggie Winkel is a director of merchandising at Nike and her knowledge about creating brand strategies is impressive. I've had the opportunity to see her explain the important role a brand plays in telling the full story of a product or service.

In her presentation, she starts by holding up three different milk chocolate bars: Hershey's, Ghirardelli, and Godiva. No matter where you're sitting, you can instantly see the difference between the three brands. The Hershey's chocolate comes in its familiar dark brown plastic wrapper with wide, silver lettering stretched horizontally across the front. The Ghirardelli bar is a bit larger and comes in a white paper wrapper. The design is vertical and starts at the top with the company's gold, blue, and white logo. In the middle is an offset photo of a square of the chocolate, with additional small pieces, including delicate chocolate curls wrapping around the edge. At the very bottom of the bar, in an elegant, curvaceous font, are the words, "Heavenly Milk Chocolate." Last but not least is the Godiva bar, its gold foil-wrapped candy distinctly showing out both ends of the bar. Its brown and gold paper wrapper is like a cummerbund with a small, festive wash of raspberry color swiping across one side.

Although these are all chocolate bars, the three are clearly not the same. Without even tasting them, you instantly get a sense of their different brands just by looking at them. But as I've said all along, the brand doesn't stop with the visual identity. And you can't have an exercise involving chocolate without tasting it. That's exactly what Maggie does next. She passes around plates of the different chocolates for a blind taste test. Everyone is encouraged to take a piece of each for a firsthand look, touch, and taste of the three brands. Once each audience member has had a chance to sample the different chocolates, Maggie has them guess which is which, based solely on taste. "Over 90 percent of the participants are able to correctly identify the chocolate," says Maggie. "Even without visual cues, the brand attributes are obvious and come through in just experiencing the products alone."

From the shape and design of the squares to the distinct flavors of the milk chocolate, each company has its own unique brand recipe, so to speak. Every detail about the chocolate bars has been carefully thought through and decisions have been made with brand clarity and intention.

"The branding voodoo that you do consists of all of those properties, everything from the exterior wrapper to the end chocolate product," says Maggie.

Each company creates a unique image and perception it wants to convey. Behind every chocolate bar, there's a big company promise of what will come, what you'll experience with that first bite—and they all hope you'll buy. And you can bet that all of their marketing activities, from PR and Website design to trade show booths and in-store displays, are also designed to reflect these brands they've worked so hard to build. And if not, they should be.

STEP 3. CREATE A MESSAGING FRAMEWORK

Beyond just a few simple words that describe your key attributes, you now need to develop your brand attributes a bit further and create some compelling messages. In the previous example about chocolate, I mentioned the "Heavenly Milk Chocolate" message on the outside wrapper of the Ghirardelli bar. This is now something the company can expand on and create more detailed messages around to use in its marketing, in everything from a press release to a Website. This could include a tagline, but a messaging framework is more of a comprehensive set of statements you use with your target audience.

I should clarify right now that taglines are important and have their place in the marketing toolkit, but, similar to a logo, they are just one tool. When I mention a tagline, I'm talking about a short, memorable phrase that sums up your company's vision or product. Just like logos, some people think messaging is all about coming up with the one, end-all, be-all tagline, but it isn't. One of the most famous taglines is Nike's: "Just do it." Another is "Got milk?" from a campaign sponsored by the California Milk Processor Board. A third example, "A mind is a terrible thing to waste," was a tagline used by the United Negro College Fund. You don't need to have a tagline, but as you start to gather words and phrases reflecting your company's brand, pay attention to any that seem to stick. If one works, use it.

A messaging framework is a set of descriptions to help bring your marketing to life. You need to find ways to convert the facts and features you sell into fascinating stories you tell. To do this, refer back to the SWOT grid you created in the last chapter. You're going to start with things you came up with as strengths and opportunities, or what you had in your "pros" column. Then, you're going to put yourself in your customers' shoes and turn that list of facts into benefits. We're so good at rattling off long lists of who we are and what we do, it can take a little time to shift our communication style and start talking about the value of these things to customers, but I'll show you how.

Here's an example. I was working with Karri, the solo owner of a boutique nail salon. She was in desperate need of boosting her customer base but wasn't sure where to start. Karri's challenge was that she had a strong brand story but wasn't communicating it. Here's what I mean. When I started working with her, she rattled off an impressive bio. She had nearly 20 years in the personalized care industry and had founded her salon in 2000. She had worked hard to position herself as a leader in her field. Her nail work had been featured in print and broadcast commercials and she made sure her business regularly won awards for giving the best manicures and pedicures in the state.

In addition to her professional credentials, Karri set herself apart from her competitors on several levels. Unlike other nail salons filled with fumes and dust from acrylic nail service, Karri only uses all-natural products personalized for her eco- and health-conscious clients. Her vision was to raise the sustainability standards in the beauty industry, and she was on a mission to bring more awareness to the benefits of natural nail care. Karri regularly invests her personal time and resources by participating in industry classes and spa exhibitions every year. And she regularly shares her industry knowledge with customers about the potentially harmful and toxic ingredients in many beauty products used every day. On top of that, she's just plain fun to hang out with while you're getting your nails done, which is also important.

Sounds like it should be a solid business, right? But as I said, she was struggling. She wasn't using all of this compelling messaging to tell her story and position her salon as a unique place to go for all the right reasons. At the time I was working with her, her prices were a bit higher than other salons. To avoid being known merely as expensive, she needed to focus her messaging on the high quality of service her customers get. She needed to turn the fact that she'd been in business for more than 15 years into a message about being a seasoned entrepreneur whose expertise and awards make her an industry leader. That's how the art of messaging works.

Some people have a hard time doing this and have issues with tooting their own horn. They might be good at coming up with long lists of facts about their business, but when it comes to crafting a positive story, they get stuck. One way to get around this is to go back to the people who helped you come up with your initial list of complementary messages. I'm talking about your employees, VIP customers, and anyone else who regularly interacts with your business and knows your brand. See if they can help turn your list of facts and features into solution-driven statements. It should be easy for them to come up with descriptions of what it feels like to do business with you.

I suggested Karri, start asking her clients how they felt during a nail or reflexology session with her, and specifically how they benefited after the treatment. She took the advice and started to hear things such as, "I get so many compliments on my nails because the manicures you give me last so long, and rarely chip," "I love your treatments because I don't get headaches from toxic fumes like I do at other nail salons," and, "I care a lot about the environment so it feels good to get my nails done at a place that uses sustainable products."

Do you see the marketing gold hidden in all of these comments? Her clients didn't mention her rates or hours of service or the range of nail polish colors she offers. They're focused on the entire experience and how her treatments make them feel. The comments are packed with insight and juicy details about the *real* value Karri delivers: the benefits of using her services and how good she makes her client feel. Now she can use these messages to strengthen her brand and tell a much more compelling story about her business.

These types of messages from customers are extremely valuable because they can go right into your marketing activities. You can start using them in your e-mail newsletters and including them on your Website. And be sure to mention them when you're interviewed by a reporter (these are all things we'll talk about more in the coming chapters). But in order to use these messages, you need to take all of this goodness and roll it into a format you can use. I suggest you create a straightforward table similar to the following and list your business's facts and features in one column on the left and your related branding messages (or what are called "value proposition statements") in the column to the right.

Product or Service: Fact and Feature List	Brand: Value and Solution Story
All products are Paraben-free and nail lacquers are "three free"—no Toluene, Formaldehyde, or Dibutyl Phthalates	Cares about your health and the environment
Nail services last for weeks without chipping	Make fewer trips to the salon and save money on high-quality treatments
Worked as director of education for nail spa; Offers advanced training for top-rated spas and salons; placed first in state for best manicures and pedicures	A seasoned expert and true industry leader

"Now I realize *I* am my brand," says Karri. "Everything from the words I choose to use to explain what I do, the manner in which I dress, the visual journey the public takes when visiting my Website, and even when they see my A-board (sandwich) sign on the sidewalk, it all needs to work together and complement what customers feel and see the minute they walk in my door."

STEP 4. PRODUCE A SET OF MULTIMEDIA BRANDING GUIDELINES

Most companies that have done their branding homework use the information they've gathered to develop a set of branding guidelines, or what's often called their branding blueprint or bible. It is literally a print and/or online handbook that outlines how your brand will be used in all marketing communication situations. This would incorporate the branding message table I just presented but goes further to give you structure and guidance for other aspects of your brand as well. Depending on how they are designed and made available, branding guidelines help everyone, from a new employee to a customer wanting to communicate about the brand.

I recently came across the guidelines for Twitter, posted on the company's Website.[5] They've designed the branding document to help people easily use their information without having to talk to their lawyers, and it's also in place to ensure any marketing done by others is consistent and correct. Their guidelines explain how to use their logos and icons on everything from Websites and T-shirts to references in books. They provide 10 different logos and explain how to use different ones, depending on the background image's color. With brand guidelines like these in place, you help everyone in and out of your organization follow the same rules and communicate the brand in a consistent way.

Managing a brand is not an easy task, and consistency issues affect both small and large companies. Your brand can get out of hand with people all over the place doing and saying the wrong things about your organization. I saw this happen a few times when I worked at Microsoft even though the company had a talented corporate branding team and a good set of guidelines. With hundreds of different products and services being marketed around the world at any given time, it was challenging for this team to monitor what I call the "umbrella" Microsoft brand. Each sub-brand had its own unique set of branding guidelines. On one end of the spectrum was Xbox, with its edgy image and controversial ads. On the opposite end you'd find the Office suite of products, with traditional messaging and marketing focused on themes of productivity. It didn't matter where the sub-brand landed; it just needed to fall under that umbrella with a dotted line up to support the main Microsoft brand.

That didn't always happen. Back when MSN 8 launched, the product marketing team decided to do something different to promote the new Internet service. The product's logo was a multicolored butterfly and its tagline read, "It's better with the Butterfly." In addition to TV ads featuring people dressed up as purple butterflies helping people to navigate the Web, the MSN group decided to hold a massive publicity stunt that kicked off in New York. The MSN 8 Butterfly Squad, as it was called, would begin its journey there and continue across the country to Los Angeles, doing good things such as visiting kids at Boys & Girls Clubs along the way.[6]

But a few days after the launch, a headline in *The New York Times* read, "City Officials Tell Microsoft to Get Its Butterfly Decals out of Town."[7] What went wrong? Part of the stunt included hiring teams of temporary staff to dress up as butterflies and rollerblade around the city, sharing promotional stickers. In their excitement to build buzz about the brand, the temps covered Manhattan sidewalks, doors, traffic signs, and planters with large adhesive butterflies, 12 to 20 inches wide.

The stunt was considered "corporate graffiti," and as a result of the defacing of public property, New York's legal counsel sent a letter to Microsoft, instructing the company to immediately remove the decals from city property. It warned that any further placement of the brightly colored butterfly stickers might lead to monetary damages or even criminal prosecution. Did this branding snafu ruin Microsoft? Absolutely not. But it didn't help the company's image (perceived by some at the time as being arrogant and monopolistic).[8] Even with preapproved permits in hand, the company brand was not positioned well in and out of New York. This is why you have to constantly monitor and manage your brand.

Since then, Microsoft has worked hard to renew its brand and use it to support the company's vision, mission, and values regarding helping people and businesses around the world realize their full potential.[9] Microsoft is doing this by reflecting that brand in all of its marketing activities, from Internet Explorer TV commercials to its Corporate Citizenship activities in Hong Kong.[10]

Had the Microsoft corporate branding team been more strict in enforcing the umbrella brand, perhaps the butterfly incident could've been avoided. But, similar to the Gap example I shared at the start of this chapter, the public's impression of a brand involves far more than just a logo or stickers. I share this Microsoft story to remind you of how important it is to have branding guidelines that go beyond just the visual aspects of your marketing. You promote your business and communicate your services in many different ways. You need to think through every scenario involving how your brand will interact with customers. What does your staff say when greeting a customer at your reception desk? What should your voice mail message be? What does your booth look like at a trade show, and what do you say to people as they walk by? What image does your corporate vehicle convey? What do you wear to a meeting with a client? How do you communicate about your competitors? Do you send thank-you notes, and if so, are they paper or e-mail? How should you train temporary employees to accurately represent your brand? Imagine every possible way you have to market and communicate your organization. How do you want to tell your story? And perhaps even more importantly, what can you do to help others spread the word and the share the right information about your brand?

Beyond that, remember to think of your brand as you would your own personality, and understand it will likely evolve in time. A woman who loves wearing jeans with heels in her 20s might prefer skirts and flats in her 60s. Just keep monitoring your core brand attributes from inside and out and adjust them as needed. Keep your guidelines updated and reflective of current times and conditions. Your personality changes as a result of your life experience and environment; if all goes well, at every stage of your life you learn and grow and continue to have an interesting story to tell. Your business's brand and supporting marketing messages and activities should evolve, too.

Once you have defined your brand and established your guidelines, then what do you do with it? Your next step is to share it with the public, to make sure everyone is communicating about you the way you want them to. For example, if a customer is having a dinner party and telling a friend about your bookstore, what do you think he's saying? You need to give your customers the information you want them to use and make it easy for them to share your stories. Make it easy for them to accurately sing your praises. This is exactly what I'll focus more on in the next chapter.

The Marketing Mindset

Take a few minutes to reflect on what you've read in this chapter and answer the following questions.

1. What are at least five words or attributes that accurately describe your brand, or the "personality" of your business?

2. How do you think the public and/or your current customers describe you?

3. Whom can you contact to gather a fresh perspective about your brand?
   - Staff
   - Customers
   - Neighboring businesses
   - Colleagues
   - Partners
   - Others

4. What elements do you already have in place as part of your branding toolkit?
   - Logo
   - Tagline
   - Messaging
   - Others

5. Make a list of all the ways you currently communicate your brand to your customers. Items might include:
   - Website
   - Mobile app
   - Facebook
   - Brochures
   - Voice mail
   - Uniform
   - Trade show booth
   - Online video

CHAPTER 4

Find Your Market

ONE OF MY ABSOLUTE, hands-down favorite clients to work with was a chocolate truffle company. And here's why: I'm a chocoholic and my clients would bring a huge bag of their truffles to just about every one of our client meetings. My business partner at the time, Stephanie Rowland, was on the Atkins diet and carefully counting carbs, so I had the sweet treats all to myself. Their product clearly wasn't their problem. The candies they produced were some of the most delicious chocolates I've ever tasted. The problem was their marketing. They had too much perishable inventory sitting around. They needed more customers.

The business was owned by a mother-daughter team, and in our very first meeting, they cut to the chase about their business goals: "We're really struggling financially and we've got to make more money soon." Apart from selling truffles to some friends and family members, they had a few wholesale opportunities, but that was it. They were already strapped for cash so didn't have much left for marketing. That's why they were hiring us. They needed a lot of help and results—fast.

As we continued on in the meeting, they had a lot of ideas. Good ideas. But before we spent too much time on the fun stuff—the cool, creative marketing activities—I backed them up. I wanted to know more about their target market. "Who are your customers?" I asked. Without missing a beat they chimed back, "People who like chocolate!" And this was their problem.

Do you see the issue with their answer? Maybe not yet, but I'll quickly explain why their response raised a red flag for me. On the surface, this seems like an obvious question. Of course your target market is going to be made up of people who like your product or service—in this case, chocolate. But this is a *huge* group of people. According to the World Cocoa Foundation, people enjoy chocolate in thousands of different forms, consuming more than 3 million tons of cocoa beans annually.[1] That's a massive number of people to have to reach with your marketing messages.

It can be done. Large companies used to reach broad audiences all the time through a process called "spray and pray." They would plaster fliers around town or do a mass direct mail campaign (spray) and hope someone would take notice (pray) and buy their product. For example, in 1968, Hershey Foods Corporation announced plans for a nationwide consumer advertising campaign spearheaded by the famous Ogilvy & Mather ad agency. Just a few years earlier, in 1963, the Hershey Chocolate Corporation purchased the H.B. Reese Candy Company. Starting with a national Sunday newspaper supplement in July 1970, followed two months later by national television and radio commercials, the campaign was an immediate success. Sales of Reese's Peanut Butter Cups and Hershey's Kisses, in particular, rose dramatically.[2]

In the good old days it wasn't always such a daunting task to reach a broad market. In many cases, marketing was more manageable, even for a small business. If you had a candy shop on Main Street, you knew exactly who in town shopped in your store, if they preferred dark, milk, or white chocolate, and whether or not they liked it with nuts. But today, with the impact of the Internet and smart, mobile devices, you have endless ways to reach people in your city as well as around the world. With this ultimate accessibility comes the unrealistic perception—and pressure—that you need to reach that huge potential market of *all* people who like chocolate. The good news is, you don't need to, and you shouldn't. The number is too overwhelming and you can't set a realistic goal, let alone a SMART objective. You'll end up spreading too thin and feeling frustrated that you're not making any progress. Even though the Cowtown Candy Company in Cody, Wyoming has a Website, that doesn't mean it's trying to sell its goodies to everyone in the world who likes sweets.[3]

TARGET AND NICHE MARKETS

As I've done in previous chapters, I want to start by clarifying up front what some of the terms I'm going to use mean. So far in the book, I've talked about your audience or market, describing your customers, your clients, your members. The broad group of people you most want to reach.

Your *target* audience or market is a specific group of these customers, and you can break them down even further into *niche* audiences or markets, which are subsets of the original target market. You create niches by discovering even more narrowly or well-defined groups of your customers. In some ways, the process of identifying niche markets in your customer base is like slicing pieces of a pie: When you break your audience down into smaller groups, they're a lot easier to fit on your marketing plate.

At first it was hard for the truffle company to identify its niche markets. In some ways it's much easier to picture a large group of potential customers instead of trying to narrow them down. But the best thing you can do to make your marketing as effective as possible is take a very close look at the individuals you're trying to reach. It may sound counterintuitive, but in order to do this, you first take a close look at your organization itself. That's right, before you can start sharing your marketing messages and news, you have to take time to put your best brand forward and pull together the stories that will resonate the most with your customers. You do this by once again building upon your vision, strengths, opportunities, and brand attributes, and then you start telling your story.

CREATING CUSTOMER SEGMENTS

I want to focus on the truffle company again for a minute, and I want you to pay close attention as I share more details about its story. I'll start by describing the two owners. As I mentioned, it was a small, family business run by a mother-daughter team. The mom, who was in her late 40s, was the keeper of the recipe and the sole crafter of the truffles. The daughter, in her mid 20s, did everything else. Her roles ranged from operations and inventory management to business development, marketing, and sales. Neither one had ever been in the business of making candy, so they were new to the industry. Their main sales came from friends and family members for parties and special occasions.

Now, I want to shift gears and focus in on my favorite part of the story: Those delicious truffles. One of the first things I noticed was that the chocolates were huge. These were not your average gumball-sized truffles, but more the size of a mandarin orange. The packaging was also unique. The handcrafted candies were individually wrapped in beautiful colored foils to reflect the variety of flavors: Green foil for the chocolate mint truffle, purple for raspberry, a distinctive copper-colored foil for mocha, and so forth. They were then placed in a long, narrow, rectangular box containing one of each of the 10 flavors. They used fresh, local ingredients and tried to support organic producers as much as possible.

After processing those additional details about the company, owners, and products, now who do you think their customers are? Still think they need to reach everyone in the world who likes chocolate? Definitely not. This is where the process of figuring out your niche markets gets fun. You get to start carving out and identifying various customer segments. And just like a pie, no slice is exactly alike. There might be a few commonalities that overlap, but each section is distinct.

I want to walk you through the process, step by step. The first thing you need to do is start with that big group. In this case, it would be all the chocolate lovers in the world. Sometimes if I'm doing this exercise in a workshop, I'll show a huge, blank circle on the screen or draw one on the whiteboard. This circle represents everyone in your main customer base.

Now I want you to do what the truffle company did and think about a big, massive, crazy-huge target market. If you own a pet store, you would be targeting all pet owners. An accountant? It would be all of the people who need help with taxes. Online magazine? People who like to read. Start with the entire pie first. Go back to your original vision if you need to. Dream big. Create a huge, delicious market pie.

Next, you start drawing lines through the pie to carve out sections that represent different groups of people who resonate with your different messages. For example, some chocolate-loving customers might be interested in trying the truffles because they value the fact that it's a family-run business. Another slice of their market might be people who support women-owned businesses or the fact that it is a small business. Still others might appreciate the artisan aspect of the candy and that it was made by hand. They get their own slice.

Someone else might feel strongly about the sustainability message and that only local, organic ingredients were used. Another might value giving distinct gifts and appreciate that the candies came in a cool package. You slice and slice, carving up that original target market until you can slice no more and not a morsel is left!

You should try to get at least three groups, but most people come up with a lot more when they do this exercise. This is exactly where your organizational brand attributes line up with your customers' needs and values.

Once you've created all these unique segments, it's helpful to get even more detailed within each one. One way to do so is to start with the basic demographic information for each. What is the age of the people in that particular segment? What's their gender? Ethnicity? Where do they live? Do they own their homes? Are they employed?

The next step is to dig even deeper. Really get into their lifestyles through their hearts and minds. What are their hobbies? Do you know what cars they drive or if they take the bus? Do they prefer to read books or blogs? Do they have kids? Can you find out if they are active in politics?

Another method for doing this is to describe what you know about an existing customer in particular from head to toe. If you're in startup mode and don't have any customers yet, you have the fun job of creating an ideal customer persona. All you need to do is come up with a picture of the person you want to do business with—the person who needs your product or service. Stacey Anderson is in this position. She's the publisher of a new magazine called *Getting Organized Magazine* and is working hard to build a base of readers and subscribers. Stacey started in the field as a professional organizer and her first marketing efforts for the magazine were directed at other organizers. To grow the magazine, she now needs to expand beyond that market and reach a different customer segment: busy, unorganized moms.

Here are some of the details Stacey uses to describe her desired customer (I'll call her Marie) from head to toe:

> *Marie is 35 to 55 years old, married, and with kids. She is self-employed or works part-time out of her home office. She is always looking for the latest gadget to help her get organized and often shops at places such as Target, The Container Store, and Bed Bath & Beyond. She likes to stay connected with her family and friends through social media tools such as Facebook and Pinterest. She enjoys reading magazines full of tips and advice, such as* Real Simple, Better Homes and Gardens, *and* O: The Oprah Magazine. *Marie has a tough time dealing with all of the paper in her house—mail, receipts, kids' calendars, things like that—and she struggles with time management and staying on top of all of her e-mail.*

She may not have a lot of readers yet, but Stacey has clearly done her homework and has come up with a lot of information about whom she's targeting. She can then use these details to create marketing activities that will effectively reach someone like Marie. This is the power of knowing your brand and using data about your customer segments to move your business forward.

CUSTOMER RELATIONSHIP MANAGEMENT

It's one thing to know this information; it's another to actually document it and use it to move you forward. This process is called Customer Relationship Management (CRM), and there are a lot of great CRM tools on the market today that can help you manage your customer data. I've worked with organizations that use everything from an Excel spreadsheet to a product called Sage ACT!. These database tools allow you to log and manage nearly every detail you can think of about your customers: dates you interacted with them, purchase history, birthdays—you name it and you can track it. Social media is rapidly changing the way we interact with customers, and with the increase in online communities, the business world is starting to pay attention. Some of the best contact management tools merge with social networks to help companies develop and manage even stronger connections with customers. Tools such as Salesforce.com can help you tap into all of the information your customers are sharing online about your brand in their conversations and feedback. In store or online, there's a way to create a profile and manage a relationship with your customers to support their buying decisions.

At the end of the day, it doesn't matter how you capture this information, you just need to do something with it. One of the biggest mistakes I see businesses make is investing a lot of money and time up front in one of these systems and then not following up by using it. Don't make the process too complicated. I don't care what you read or research or hear from a colleague, if it's easier for you to manage your top three segments in a paper notebook, do it. If you have a sales team and can invest in setting up Salesforce.com, do it. Use a process that will help you gather the information you need to tell your story to the right people.

The more information you can gather about your niche customers, the better you can target your marketing activities to not only reach them, but also resonate with them. You're now discovering as many unique customer details or "ingredients" as you can within each slice of your original pie. There might be some overlap in your segments, and that's just fine. You may find one niche segment is made up of men and women who listen to the radio, or another segment might include kids ages 5 through 10, as well as teenagers who still like reading books instead of reading online.

HOW DO YOU FIND INFORMATION ABOUT A TARGET MARKET?

One question that usually comes up at this point is, "So how do I find all of this information about my customers?" Great question. There are a few ways to get it. Some of it may have come out when you did your SWOT analysis back in Chapter 2. Sometimes you may see it and experience it firsthand when you interact with your customers. For example, maybe a client mentions she was reading the local business journal, or a supporter of your nonprofit mails in her donation with a breast cancer awareness sticker on the outside of the envelope. Maybe in the comments section of your blog a majority of your readers describe their political views. The details about your customers' stories are often right within reach if you look and listen.

A great example of an organization that was able to narrow down its broad customer market and find information about a specific segment to target is a church management software company. A colleague of mine, Matt Heinz, owns Heinz Marketing and was helping the business find better ways to market and sell its solutions across the country. "They originally wanted to go after every church in America, but I told them if they wanted to increase their chances of success, they'd have to scale down their approach," says Matt. In order to do this, Matt came up with some criteria. If the church didn't have a good handle on technology, there would be a pre-existing hurdle to convincing them to buy the software. Matt says, "It came down to asking, 'Do they have a Website, yes or no?' That one, simple question ruled out a bunch right there. And then we looked at things such as church size, growth rate, and denomination. We found much of this information online or with the help of a few strategically placed phone calls."

Through this process of segmenting, Matt was able to help his client identify the best potential customers: largely non-denominational churches experiencing high growth who were already using technology in innovative ways. They had real data-management issues and were much more likely to buy the software and service. Doing this work up front and profiling specific niches in the broad market helped Matt's clients get significantly higher responses to marketing activities than they would have without the profiling.

Detailed information about clients is in many ways much easier for a brick-and-mortar or service-based business to gather than it is for an organization based solely online. Here's why: Amazon may know the books I've purchased in the past, but, the manager at Ravenna Third Place Books, an independent book store, knows much more about the rest of me. He knows I have a cat, am recovering from plantar fasciitis after a week of over-exercising, want to be a better cook, like hearing lectures, am an extrovert, and can't get enough cupcakes and Indian food. Does any of that information help him recommend a new book when he sees me in his store? Definitely.

WHAT IF YOU HAVE NO MARKET YET—OR WANT TO CHANGE YOUR TARGET MARKET?

No customers yet? This can be really challenging. You don't have customers to talk to and you're just starting to create a community online. But all is not lost. There's still hope! You can do a couple of things.

As I said earlier, you can start by making one up. Who is your hypothetical customer, or better yet, who is your dream customer? If you could have anyone come into your store or visit your site, who would it be? One way to start building your target market is to look at who is doing business with your competitors. Is there a gap in the market that you're able to fill? Go look at businesses similar to yours online. Read their customer testimonials and reviews. See what people like and don't like.

For example, in my neighborhood there are three sushi restaurants within five blocks. If you wanted to open another sushi restaurant in that same location, even if it's going to be completely radical in product and concept, you could learn a lot about your potential market from reading the customer feedback on your competitors' Websites, checking out their customer comments posted on review sites such as Urbanspoon.com, Yelp.com, and Citysearch.com, and reading old-school newspaper restaurant reviews.

Speaking of old school, you can also do some undercover sleuthing and just go in and enjoy a sashimi plate and observe the customers. Be a secret shopper of sorts and ask the waiter as many questions as possible. If that makes you uncomfortable, you can ask one of your employees or even a friend to do it. And there are of course consultants you can hire to provide official secret shopper services and competitive research.

It also helps to look at what's happening in your industry and your professional organizations. Talk to people. Attend a trade show. Get support from your chamber of commerce, the Small Business Administration, or your merchant association. You could do a test market focus group, send out a survey, or go to your local library. All of the techniques and tools I discussed in Chapter 2 for your SWOT analysis would be just as effective in researching your target market, too. The possibilities are endless. Just be sure to build upon your brand as you begin to define your customer base. People will listen when you start telling your story.

What if you want to change customers? Or dump the ones you have? No problem. I know that sounds harsh, but I worked with a photographer who was terrific at weddings, but wanted to shift to a different market. Her background was in photojournalism and she wanted to bring this aspect of photography to her family portrait and wedding business. Unfortunately, it meant her rates would go up as she would need to spend a lot more time observing the bride and groom to capture their special day in her unique way. It would require not only a different pricing model and process, but also a completely different way of telling her story. Not all of her original clients would be interested in continuing to work with her. As she converted her business model, she would need to find new people and let some of the old people go. She'd have to find some new slices to add to the empty wedges in her pie.

TAILOR YOUR MARKETING TO YOUR NICHES

Once you have your target market and niche audiences defined, when you really know your main customer segments, you can start your marketing! You begin listening to what they want and giving them what they need! Different customers will care about different things, so there's a good chance you need to create a variety of marketing messages. You will be slicing and dicing your story, sharing different pieces with different customers. You start by picking one of your niche markets, and then move on to the next.

Going back to the truffle company example, we identified three niche segments of customers: local boutique hotels, local restaurants, and executive assistants at local corporations. You can see that there were even more important details to uncover within each of these three defined groups. For example, we needed to find hotels that put chocolate on pillows, restaurants with sustainable, organic menus, and assistants who needed high-end gifts for their managers' clients.

After we had these details, we began to create different messages that would resonate with these groups of customers. Instead of bombarding them with facts and features about the chocolates, we had to tell a story about how the truffles would benefit them, add value to their organizations, and ultimately make their lives better. For the hotels and restaurants, we decided to play up the messages about the organic ingredients and artisan process. For the executive assistants, we focused on the high-end packaging and artisan process. The hotels and restaurants would need simple, one-page fact sheets that the truffle company owner would drop off in person, along with a few free samples. The best way to reach the executive assistants was to e-mail them and invite them to a free tasting event. We'll talk about how you create an actual action plan in future chapters, but this is how you begin to mix and match your messages and tell your story effectively to your target market.

This goes for service-based businesses, too. For example, if I'm delivering a keynote to corporate types and senior banking executives, I tend to share more of my professional stories from Microsoft. If I'm leading a workshop for small business owners, I highlight examples from my years managing my family business and working with entrepreneurs.

A unique story about a group working hard to tailor its marketing activities to its customer segments is PACOS Trust, an NGO in Malaysia. The community-based, volunteer-run organization is dedicated to empowering indigenous communities in the Sabah region of Malaysia, located on the northern portion of the island of Borneo. I was introduced to the region, as well as the organization, when I was invited to serve as a speaker through the U.S. State Department. Sabah is one of the most remarkable places I've ever been, full of beautiful national parks, rivers, mountains, wildlife reserves, jungle terrain, and beaches. Yet while the interior region remains sparsely populated with only villages, development is happening rapidly throughout the region and encroaching upon the natural lands and their inhabitants.

To address these sustainability issues, Anne Lasimbang, the executive director of PACOS, is working hard to run multiple programs ranging from land rights to resource management. An example of a program that has helped move the organization forward is its community education program. This program provides early childcare and education to rural communities in Sabah. "On the surface, it might seem ordinary and small, but it has positioned PACOS as one of the most respected NGOs in Malaysia," says Anne. In order for the program to be successful, PACOS needed to recruit women deep in the rural villages and help empower them to be community leaders. This was no easy task, as most of the women were illiterate and lacked confidence. In addition, the messages used by PACOS needed to be rooted in the people's indigenous culture or they would not resonate.

PACOS took all of this into careful consideration by creating relevant marketing activities and promotional material. PACOS couldn't send e-mails or put up fliers because the women were unable to read and write and had no access to technology in their villages. Instead, the organization had to rely on word-of-mouth efforts. Creating compelling photo exhibits during community events allowed the organization to appeal to the women on an emotional level and reach this targeted segment of its customer base. "Once the women gained information and confidence, they were able to do something for themselves as well as for their community," says Anne. "One example is the women's group in Kipouvo; they undertook a village community homestay program. Through the children's program these women became organized and their activities have evolved."

One year, PACOS partnered with Camps International, a volunteer tourism company based in the UK to bring clients into Sabah. "Kipouvo village was one of the destinations, and in a year they earned MYR $45,000 [USD $12,000]. This was truly an achievement for this group of rural women." As this story illustrates, when it comes to your target market, the best way to reach your goals and move your business forward is to slice and dice your stories and messages to match the needs of the audience at hand.

THE PROS AND CONS OF NICHES

In some cases, narrowing your focus can seem as though you're limiting your options. It can also be challenging to have to pick which customers to focus on and which ones to set aside. I experienced this early in my career. The process reminded me of those painful times in junior high when I wasn't one of the first chosen to be on the dodgeball team. I didn't want to do that to my customers, and I wanted my messages, my story, to resonate with all of my clients, from the small businesses to the nonprofits to the artists to the government agencies to the schools to the corporations—all of them. I didn't want to lock my consulting services into just one of those categories. But eventually I realized it wasn't about me.

To better explain this, I thought it would be helpful to share a point of view from Barry Mitzman, an expert on communications strategy and messaging. I first worked with him more than a decade ago when he was vice president of SS+K, a marketing communications firm that served some of Microsoft's groups; then again when he was director of strategic communications at Microsoft; and yet again at Seattle University, where he is now professor of strategic communications and director of the university's Center for Strategic Communications.

The key to telling your story effectively, he says, is to get over yourself. That is, stop thinking about your own needs and wants for at least a moment. Think instead about the people you're trying to reach. What do *they* need and want? How are those needs and wants served by your story, product, service, or organization? First, figure out how to be *relevant*. Then, forge that connection to your target audiences by honing a few simple, key messages—ideas critically important for you to get across and also potentially important to your target audiences based on what they already know and believe. "In a sense, effective, persuasive communication is very Zen," says Barry. "To win, you must let go of your ego."

He's right. What I finally realized, and what's so amazing about the process of defining niche customer markets, is that it does the opposite of what you might think. Instead of restricting your options, it expands them and allows you to have tremendous freedom within each segment. If you focus your efforts on exactly whom you need to reach, you realize the size of your original pie stays the same; you're not losing anything. All those little niches still add up to one big pie; you're just giving a few defined customer groups the attention they need. In fact, the size of your market doesn't change at all, but by delivering more customized marketing to each niche, you're packing more revenue opportunities into each slice.

In addition to a sense of feeling limited, some people get overwhelmed at the thought of dividing their customer base into segments. They're worried that by creating so many different customer niches they'll get spread too thin and will not have enough time or budget to manage them all. That's a valid concern, which is why I suggest you pick no more than about three to five to focus on at any one time, depending on your time and resources.

Think about it. If you go back to the pie analogy, you *could* cut a pie into 16 mini pieces, but as I can attest to on Thanksgiving Day, that's just too small of a serving. Then you aren't giving your customers all of the information they need or the attention they deserve. Mayna Sgaramella McVey started her wardrobe consulting business, Closet Fly, in 2005. Since then, she's helped a diverse group of men and women look amazing regardless of their size, shape, age, or budget. In order to market her business effectively, she's focused on one broad customer market: women in a life transition. That doesn't mean she won't work with men, but the majority of her clients are women so she makes sure her marketing efforts resonate with them.

Throughout the years, Mayna has carved out five niche customer segments:

1. **New moms:** Women in this phase of their life have gone through a major life change and Mayna knows how to help them feel good and dress for their new body, whether they were able to get back to that pre-baby size or not.

2. **Empty nesters or retirees:** When their kids leave home, many women finally start thinking about themselves again and start buying new clothes. Mayna also works with retirees who have closets full of professional suits but no longer need them. Even a midlife physical change such as menopause may lead to wardrobe adjustments if a woman is experiencing physical changes such as hot flashes.

3. **Professionals:** "These are women who have either switched to a different profession or moved up in their position at work," says Mayna. "They used to dress casually and now need to upgrade their wardrobe for work, or the opposite, in the case where they left a corporate job and are now self-employed and have more wardrobe options."

4. **Weight changers:** Mayna also targets women who just lost or gained weight from either a health issue or because they've started a new diet or exercise program. "In both cases, their weight has changed and they need help dressing their new size and learning how to dress their shape."

5. **Divorcees:** "These are the women who may be on the market again and want to feel good," says Mayna. "They've gone through a painful process and want to feel better about themselves and feel sexy again; they are ready for a lifestyle change, and that includes their appearance."

The number of slices you create in your pie depends on your time and resources, but if five work for Mayna, that might be a perfect number of niche markets for you as well.

At the end of the day, you can see that the pros far outweigh the cons when it comes to slicing and dicing your target market. This process allows you to tailor your messaging and your activities so they resonate with the right eyes and ears, and you get better results. All of this information, these details you gather about who your customers really are, is invaluable. When you have this much data to work with, it will make your marketing much easier and more effective. By being more selective about what parts of your story you want to tell and to whom you want to tell it, you'll get faster results.

The Marketing Mindset

Take a few minutes to reflect on what you've read in this chapter and answer the following questions:

1. Whom would you describe as your broadest base of customers? If it helps, draw a big, empty circle. Who fills up the entire pie?

2. Describe one of your customers—or a desired customer— from head to toe. Fill in as many details as possible. Here is a list to start the process:

   ⇒ Age

   ⇒ Location

   ⇒ Ethnicity

   ⇒ Gender

   ⇒ Political status

➠ Employment status

➠ Family status

3. Based on the information you came up with for #2, create three to five niche customer segments. What elements distinguish each of these groups?

4. Play the mix-and-match game. Match your messages to the appropriate audience. Who needs to hear what part of your story?

5. Do you have a CRM process? If so, how could it be improved? If not, what method could you use to improve how you track and use your customer data?

PART III

STRENGTH:
Boost Your Efforts by Extending Your Reach

No one can whistle a symphony. It takes a whole orchestra to play it.
—H.E. Luccock

Up until this point in the book, you've looked inward to find the best strategies for your marketing, as well as viewed the landscape to see where and how your products and services fit. You've learned more about how to brand your offerings and narrowed your audience to be able to deliver a compelling message to exactly the right people. That's no small task, and in this third section of the book, I'll explain why you don't have to do everything on your own. The power of your marketing is made much greater by building a virtual team of your customers, partners, and opinion influencers (such as the media)—all of which are external forces that can help extend the reach of your marketing.

In Chapter 5, I'll explain the customer relationship cycle and you'll learn how to create more effective and authentic interactions with your customers. When you approach customers as brand ambassadors and an extension of your business, you strengthen your marketing muscle and improve the chances of them helping to promote your organization.

Chapter 6 looks at the power of partnerships and alliances. It may sound counterintuitive, but there are ways you can collaborate with your competitors to strengthen your marketing efforts and better serve your customers. I'll show you creative examples of how this is done, as well as explore other types of partnerships that will help you move forward.

In Chapter 7 you'll get an overview of how to create and strengthen relationships with different types of media outlets, and how to make your public relations (PR) efforts more effective. These tried-and-true ways still work today, even though the media world is undergoing radical changes. Here you'll also learn how to integrate traditional PR with social media activities.

In these chapters, you'll learn how to amp up your marketing by creating programs with three powerful groups: your customers, your partners, and the media. With this extended reach, combined with your own skills and talents, you'll be able to accomplish so much more than what you could ever do on your own.

CHAPTER 5

Leverage Your Customers

ONE OF MY FAVORITE restaurants in the world is a place called A Taste of India. Eating there is an amazing experience. Let's start with the building itself. It's located in a yellow and white house on the corner of a busy, one-way thoroughfare, but once you step inside, you're magically transported to another place. Colorful, mirrored tapestries cover the walls, delicious smells drift from the kitchen, and there's always the soothing sound of Indian music playing in the background. If there's any sort of line, which there often is at this popular spot, you're given a free cup of the most incredible chai tea you have ever tasted.

A Taste of India is a family business run by Mohammed Arfan Bhatti and his father. Together, they have more than 30 years in the restaurant industry, and it shows. As Indian music plays quietly in the background, an abundance of staff members go above and beyond to anticipate your every dining need. The service is impeccable. And don't get me started on the food. From rich curries and creamy masalas to moist, red-orange tandoori chicken and huge, warm ovals of nan bread overflowing the edges of their baskets, there's something delectable for everyone.

Mohammed is an attentive owner, and on the nights he's managing the restaurant, he's not hiding behind the host station; he's walking the floor. He is quick to have his staff set up a table for a last-minute large party or deliver a free appetizer if the meal is running a few minutes late.

One night, after a very long and stressful day, I decided to take myself out to dinner at my favorite restaurant. I was exhausted and spent most of my meal with my nose buried in my journal. At the end of the dinner, when I was finally ready to go, I asked the waitress for the check. "There is no bill tonight," she replied with a smile. "Mohammed has covered your meal, ma'am." I was deeply shocked and pleasantly surprised. On my way out, I sought out Mohammed and thanked him profusely. When I asked what the occasion was for his generosity, he humbly replied, "You looked like you had a rough day and deserved to be treated well."

There's a reason I go back to this restaurant again and again. It's not because I expect a free meal every time. I don't. On top of a delicious meal, what Mohammed and his staff gave me that night was a positive experience I will never forget and a story I will tell again and again.

That's what this chapter is about. It's about creating incredible experiences for your customers. And as this story explains, it doesn't have to be something big; it can be something as small as a cup of chai. It's about using everything you have worked on so far to share your story with your customers and empower your customers to be your messengers and narrators.

DO YOU NEED MORE CUSTOMERS?

It doesn't matter if you run a nonprofit in Malaysia or a corporation such as Boeing—nearly every organization I've worked for, consulted with, or researched believes it desperately needs more customers. Why? Because people equate more customers with more business, and that means more revenue. The common mantra seems to be, "More, more, more!" The only people who might not be in this position are small, service-based businesses that can only take on as much client work as there are hours in the day. But once their projects are done, they've got to fill that pipeline up again.

The challenge with this is that it can be hard enough to keep the customers we have, let alone add more to the mix. If you don't do your marketing right, it will end up being ignored by tired minds, deaf ears, and judgmental eyes. There are a few reasons for this: People today are busy, bombarded, and skeptical."

1. People Are Busy.

People have a lot going on these days. Paying bills, taking care of kids, fixing the car, scheduling doctors' appointments, and remembering friends' birthdays are just some of the things they need to devote time to. It isn't easy to work your way into someone's jam-packed schedule and onto the to-do list. It used to be you could just present your information in a straightforward way. You could put up a billboard and people would see it. Run your radio ad and people would hear it. The world used to be more of a seller's market in which you had the customers in the palm of your hand. Those days are over. You've got to find ways to capture your customers' attention. The first step is to put yourself in your customers' shoes as often as possible.

2. People Are Bombarded

People are inundated with messages today. The numbers are out of control. When I last checked, the average consumer is expected to see or hear about 2 million marketing messages a year. That's more than 5,000 per day.[1] Think about it: From the time you get up in the morning and turn off your Sony alarm clock playing your local NPR news station to the time you brush your teeth with Crest, pull on your Gap pajamas, and slide into your sheets from Bed Bath & Beyond, you've been exposed to a lot of brands and a lot of marketing noise. And the apps! How could I forget the mobile apps? No human can possibly pay attention to all of this information. You've got to find a way to break through all the noise and clutter in their world.

3. People Are Skeptical

Because of time crunches and information overload, people have become very skeptical of promotional information and activities. They have to be. There's no other way to survive in our over-marketed world. Thanks to all the bad marketing out there, tolerance is at an all-time low. Customers have been hit with so much spam throughout the years that they don't hesitate to delete an unfamiliar e-mail. A large percentage of people read their paper mail over a recycling bin and immediately toss anything that isn't a bill or from a familiar source. Some direct mail experts say this number can be as high as eight out of 10 customers not reading your mailed marketing materials.[2] When it comes to TV, other than on Super Bowl Sunday, people tend to fast-forward through commercials as quickly as possible. They screen out calls to avoid salespeople who've managed to get around the national "do not call" registry, and hardly anyone answers his or her door unless it's a pizza they ordered and asked to be delivered. Customers are in the driver's seat. They're selective about what information they choose to be exposed to. Their walls are up, their eyes are covered, and their ears are plugged as they deflect unwanted marketing messages and materials.

KEEP THE ONES YOU'VE GOT

How do you get people to not only pay attention to you, but to also connect with you? How can you win them over and then persuade them to act? I know these challenges may seem daunting, but the solution is easier than you think: You start by doing more with what you have—strengthening relationships with your current base of customers. Once you've done that, the rest will come. Your customers will work as your virtual sales team and help you extend your reach, share your stories, and ultimately attract new customers.

Here's the deal: It's a lot more expensive and time-intensive to find a new customer, so the better fix is to keep the ones you've got, and create ways for them to do more business with you. So we will start there. Use the resource right at your fingertips. Share your best stories with them and watch what happens.

RELATIONSHIP CYCLE

The reason you have certain customers goes beyond just your product and services. You've created some sort of relationship with them. A big mistake many businesses have made is thinking that relationships with customers are one-way. They aren't. Today, you can't just push information out to your customers. You can't just put up a sign on the side of the street. As in any relationship, there needs to be give and take. Relationships are fluid. They can slip backwards, move forwards, or be at a standstill. And they have the potential to evolve.

This last point is key, and is a huge opportunity for organizational relationships with your customers. It helps to have a basic understanding of what's called the customer lifecycle or relationship cycle. It identifies different phases that customers tend to move through as they develop a relationship with you. Let's walk through all of the phases so you get a sense of the rhythm and flow of a relationship with your customers, clients, and supporters.

1. Know

This is where potential customers first become aware of your company and get the first taste of your brand. It could be as simple as driving by a building and seeing a sign in the window. It could be surfing the Web and coming across a Website never explored before. They haven't formed any feelings or made a judgment yet. It just exists in their minds from the first few seconds of exposure.

2. Like

This is where customers shift from being familiar with you to forming a positive image of you. It could be for any reason at all. Maybe they think you have a cool logo because it's an illustration of a red chicken and they like the color red. Maybe they click around your Website and see a member of your team who has a nice smile and think he looks like a nice guy. Feelings develop for a wide range of reasons. Your potential customers now not only know about you, but they also like you.

3. Trust

As in dating, it's one thing to think someone is nice and cute; it's another to let someone pick you up at your home on a first date. There's a level of trust that needs to be established before the relationship progresses to that next level. This is exactly what begins to happen with your customers.

They may read a positive review about your retail store on their favorite community blog. They might hear a friend talking about your accounting services and how you helped him or her get $1,000 back on an old tax return. They may move from your staff member's headshot to his bio, and see that he's got an impressive list of professional experience. Something happens in the customers' minds to give you an extra level of credibility.

4. Try

In this phase, the customers get to try a little taste of you—literally. This could be anything from a "Top 10 list" you offer as a free download on your Website, to a 15-minute informational phone call you give to prospective clients, to a free sample. This last one is what worked for me when I was passing by a new cheesecake shop called The Confectional near my home. I'd moved through the first three phases but, not being a huge cheesecake fan, had no reason to go in or make a purchase. One afternoon they were offering little bites so I tried one. Delicious!

5. Buy

Before I knew it, I was inside the tiny cheesecake boutique, learning from the staff that they use Maria biscuits from Spain to create the thick, decadent crust. And guess what? I bought some. I didn't buy a full-sized cheesecake, but I ended up taking home several of their chocolate-covered cheesecake truffles. This is what this phase is all about: getting your customers to the point at which they pay for your products. They buy your service, or donate to your charitable cause. They move beyond just a taste and swallow you, hook, line, and sinker.

6. Repeat

If you've done everything right so far, chances are good that your customers will be back for more. They will want to replicate the experience or maybe even try something new. In a small business, this is when you have the opportunity to learn your regular customers' names and begin to form a relationship. Online, if you're tracking customer data, you'll have details about the steady flow of business from these people.

7. Refer

Finally, your customers have reached the last phase, which is one of the most valuable: They are willing to put their reputation on the line and mention you to someone. It doesn't have to be someone they know. Going back to the cheesecake story, the other day I saw two people outside the door of the shop, contemplating going in. "They are really good cheese-cakes," I said as I walked by. "They even have mini truffle-sized ones if you just want to try a bite." In they went.

⫸ ⫸ ⫸

Keep in mind, this is a general overview of how customers interact with you. There are no hard and fast rules here. Some people skip through some of the phases: For example, if you are desperately in need of a toilet plunger you may go directly to the hardware store in your neighborhood, whether or not you like it, trust its reputation, or have ever shopped there before. But if you use this cycle as your guide, it can help you understand your potential market and help you create good relationships with the people who do business with you.

WHAT'S A "GOOD" RELATIONSHIP?

Everyone is buzzing about relationship marketing these days and how important it is. But no one really talks about what a relationship is, what it takes to create a good one, or, most importantly, how to sustain it and keep it going so it works for both people. A basic description of a relationship is this: *A connection between two or more parties*—but there's no reference to the quality of that relationship. This is where marketing comes into play. Marketing is all about making it worth someone's while to do business with you. It's about delivering value and real benefit. But that's hard to do when you're a business with millions of customers. It's hard to do even if you have only a few hundred customers. But here's a solution.

CONNECT WITH YOUR V.I.P.S

Most people have heard of the Pareto principle, or what's also known as the 80/20 rule. When you apply it to business, it means that in most situations, roughly 80 percent of your business comes from just 20 percent of your customers. That means you probably have a small pocket of very important people (VIPs) who are crucial to the success of your business. Like the high rollers at a casino, these are the people who spend a lot of money with you. They already know you, like you, and trust you—they may even love you!

They probably already share stories about you with their friends and family members and refer business to you all the time. They not only sign up for your e-newsletter, but they actually read it. They come to your events. They are loyal to your brand and believe in your services and products. They come back again and again. They'd do anything for you, with or without a thank-you note or gift card. The point is, if you invest more time and energy in this small group of VIPs who matter the most, you'll maximize your effort and get better results. They are one of your most powerful and effective marketing tools. If you can create more ways to connect with them or design some services just for them, they can have a powerful, positive impact on your business.

So if you aren't yet, you need to start cultivating your base of these loyal VIP customers. And I'm not just talking about setting a stack of "Buy 12 Get the 13th Free" punch cards out on your counter, although those have their place. I'm talking about really taking time to get to know your best customers, the ones who keep bringing in those cards for their 13th drink. Then, go further and do something really special and meaningful just for them.

Think about a casino as an example. Casinos give their best customers everything from penthouse suites and personal chefs to a town car and butler services. Within your industry and budget, you need to be doing the same. You need to find your best customers, acknowledge them, and thank them. Think of it this way: They are doing great things for you now; imagine what might happen if you share more of your stories with them, harness their energy and passion, and use it to take you in the direction you want to go!

Here's an example of a small marketing activity directed at a handful of VIP customers that paid off in a big way. I used to work with a top interior decorator and owner of a company called The Enhanced Home. Despite his success, he was experiencing a lull in his business due to the down economy. After clarifying his strategies and talking through some of his branding messages, we decided to find a way to help him reconnect with a handful of his very best customers, whom we determined were a mix of high-end realtors and homeowners. He was from Latin America and that was part of his story. He purchased 25 handmade, beautiful coasters. They were perfect because they represented his brand and his country, and were related to his industry of home décor. Along with the gift, he included a stylish card containing a hand-written note thanking them for their business and acknowledging how much he enjoyed working with them. The next week his phone was ringing off the hook with new projects from nearly every past client he contacted or new people they had referred to him. It resulted in close to $100,000 in revenue.

Here are a few questions to ask and things to do to start this process of cultivating and connecting with your VIPs.

1. Who Are They?

First, you need to make sure you clearly know who these customers are. This ties back to the work you did to define your target market and niche customer segments. Dig deep and figure out exactly whom you're talking to and doing business with. Adriana Medina is the owner of a gym called Fuerte Fitness. As a personal trainer, she spends every day working side by side with her clients, and as you can imagine, she knows a lot about them. This goes beyond the basics, such as knowing the types of exercise classes they like to take and equipment they prefer to use. Adriana knows her clients well enough to motivate them and keep them going through so many of life's bumps in the road. She reminds them about what's important and why they're at the gym. It might be getting them in shape for a fitness show or motivating them with enough energy and power to keep up with their kids. She listens as they share their hopes and reveal challenges; she understands their personal relationships and deepest fears. On her Website, she posts before and after photos of her clients. In their own words, she lets them describe the details behind their success stories. These stories give her a unique opportunity to learn even more about her clients and incorporate their messages into her own.

2. Where Are They?

Once you know who your customers are, then you have to figure out where they are and how to reach them. This is especially true if you're a new organization and are trying to build a base of customers. But even existing businesses need to pay close attention to where their customers spend their time. On a Saturday afternoon, are they hanging out online or do they like to read a good book in a coffee shop? Do they pick up tips and how-to information from friends on Facebook or do they prefer to learn in a classroom environment? Once you know where they are, then you can go there to talk to them. That is far easier than trying to create some new process or place for them to use. You don't need to reinvent the wheel.

3. What Do They Care About?

As business owners, what you care about is very straightforward. It's usually focused on some aspect of growth, such as boosting the bottom line, selling more products, getting more of your messages heard, making a difference, or making more money. But what about your customers? What do *they* care about, and what are *their* concerns? Often you're so focused on chattering about how great your organization is that you forget to listen to the concerns of your customers. You've put away the customer suggestion box and turned off the comments on your blog. You need to bring these powerful tools back and be completely open to feedback. That's the only way you'll gain valuable insights into your customers' priorities.

4. How Do They Want to Connect With You?

In business, too often you think you know best. You decide you should write a blog and start cranking out content and then wonder why no one comments on your articles. You invest a lot of time and effort designing e-newsletters and then wonder why they don't get read. One of the easiest ways to get to the bottom of how you should connect with your customers is to ask! Before you start creating new marketing events and investing in more brochures, find out what works for your customers. Remember how busy, bombarded, and skeptical they are; they will be honest with you.

Trophy Cupcakes is a boutique bakery packing the finest ingredients and attention to detail and artistry into each delicious, miniature confection. Their fans range from Martha Stewart, who thinks their cakes are "utterly delicious" to on-the-go moms. Trophy does a great job of listening to its customers and paying attention to how they want to interact with the company. Twitter is perfect for some of their busy customers who want to stay on top of the latest flavors and promotions. Here's a tweet from a new customer that was retweeted by Trophy:

> Finally tried @**trophycupcakes** in #**bellevue**. I devoured my Red Velvet while my bf ate his Lemon Coconut cupcake :)

> @**m_candy** Yay! So glad you made it! Happy Valentine's Day too!

Some of their other customers prefer to receive a monthly e-mail reminder to tease their sweet palette, so Trophy uses that marketing tool, too. Pay attention to what customers want and don't want when it comes to communicating with you.

5. What's in It for Them?

What motivates a person to do business with you? What's the benefit? There's always some motivation behind the action, and the sooner you can figure it out, the better. Once you know the real value your product or service holds, you can create much more effective marketing activities. For example, a fashion stylist named Angie Cox cofounded one of the top style advice sites, called YouLookFab.com. As part of her services, cofounder Greg Cox launched a very cool mobile app. Here's how it works: If you're out shopping alone and fall in love with some shoes or an item of clothing, but are unsure whether you should buy it or not, you take a picture of yourself wearing it and post it through the app for others to review. The real-time photo is posted on YouLookFab's highly engaged and supportive forum where members provide constructive, honest feedback on the photos. It's like having a virtual group of girlfriends in the store, shopping with you. On top of that, Angie adds her two cents to almost every post. And that's worth a lot because she has 20 years of experience in the business as a designer, fashion buyer, and stylist.

The app isn't free; in fact, it's a bit higher priced than most. But what customers get is an incredible experience at a great value. What's in it for Angie and Greg is this: They are providing a new service to her existing customer base, and Angie is also reaching potential new followers in an innovative way. But it only works because they are giving their subscribers something desirable. So put yourself in your customers' shoes and consider what's in it for them to do business with you. Finding their motivation is key to your marketing success.

BUILD STRONGER CONNECTIONS WITH YOUR CUSTOMERS

Once you've gathered the information in steps 1 through 5, you can start using it to give your customers a reason to do more business with you. Now you're ready to engage in some marketing activities that drive results.

Here is a list of seven ideas that might help you strengthen the connections with your customers.

1. Brag About Them

We've talked about the power of sharing your customer testimonials and even photos. If you've got an amazing customer story worth tooting your horn about, do it! One example of this is a pilates business called Studio Evolve. When rock star Sting was in Seattle on tour with his band, The Police, his handlers called around to find a pilates pro. Studio owner Martine Dedek ended up working with him for several days. She gave him the same top-notch experience she gives all of her clients, and as a result, Sting gave her something: a hand-written thank-you note:

> *Extraordinary, revolutionary, revelatory, and ultimately freeing.*
> *Highly recommend five stars.* *****

Martine earned every word of that praise and proudly has his note framed and displayed in the entry of the studio for all to see. She also used it to gain positive media coverage in the local newspaper and posted it for years on the home page of her Website to give the business instant credibility. Great customers don't have to be celebrities. Today the studio's Website is packed with positive testimonials and amazing transformational stories from its day-to-day clients. The point is, you can and should brag about any interesting customer story.

2. Surprise Them

Coastal Kitchen may seem like a typical neighborhood fish house, but it keeps its regular customers on their toes by changing things around every few months, when it rolls out a new menu focusing on the varied coastal regions around the world. But the change doesn't stop with the menu. The art adorning its walls made by local artists rotates with each new menu, and even the bathrooms reflect the cultural change. As you enter the powder room you're greeted with a recorded story filled with interesting tidbits and language lessons for the region. If your customers love surprises and are never sure what they'll find, they just might keep coming back.

3. Impress Them

Speaking of celebrities, some customers like doing business with cool people and award-winning businesses. Like it or not, that's just the way the world works. If your customers are impressed with credentials, and you've earned them, use them to your advantage. One example of this is publicist Kristen Graham. She represents some of the top chefs in the country, and as a result of her hard work, she's been able to get her clients featured in major media outlets including *Esquire* magazine, *The New York Times*, and the *Martha Stewart Show*. She proudly lists the logos of these outlets on her site where her potential clients can see them. Many businesses are far too humble and keep that praise and good news in a folder. If you've got the credentials, show them off! Your customers might be even more thrilled to do business with you.

4. Entertain Them

Who doesn't like a party? Okay, some introverts out there might not, but even my introverted friends are always glad they went to an event after the fact. Girl Power Hour is a great example of how to "professionally" party with your customers. It was started by Darnell Sue, and each month she brings hundreds of young professional women together for a different twist on the humdrum networking hour. There are always goody bags packed with tangible, valuable things her customers actually want, such as copies of *Glamour* magazine, perfume samples, and bite-sized energy bars. The point is to bring charity, empowerment, and social glam to networking, and she does it with swanky cocktails and hip DJs. Of course, behind the scenes she is building her brand and business, but doing it under the guise of a party—and her customers love it!

5. Make Things Easy for Them

Launched in 2010, *JENESEQUA Style* is the first online magazine *and* independent style publisher for the iPad and iPhone. Founding editor in chief Melissa Middleton launched JENESEQUA.com (JNSQ) to serve as an innovative forum for all things stylish. She knows success lies in making her exquisite content easily available to her current and potential readers. In order to keep her readers engaged and on top of trends, Melissa recruited an all-star editorial staff from across the globe. Each contributor is an accomplished blogger with a unique voice and area of expertise to share with readers. Together, they define JNSQ's holistic approach to style and to life: chic, approachable, and always memorable.

"Each of our articles is enhanced with YouTube videos, Pinterest boards, photo galleries, and Websites curated by hand, allowing our readers to engage with more content without having to do any extra work," says Melissa. In order to enhance the JNSQ reader experience, Melissa hired a company called RepublicofApps to quickly create one-of-a-kind iPad and iPhone apps with simple interfaces to ensure her content was easy to access on mobile devices. The apps also let readers save their favorite articles and images to a personal profile for offline reading and archiving. Melissa continues to evolve the technology and use these apps to make style approachable and easy for her readers.

6. Help Them

Sometimes what you have to offer your customers isn't easy to talk about. Amy Lang is in that position. She founded Birds + Bees + Kids to help parents become informed, confident, and comfortable talking to their children about love and relationships. Because she knows talking to kids about sex isn't easy and can be just as embarrassing for the parents as it is for the kids, she offers her customers access to her workshops via live video feed from the comfort of their homes. In a safe, anonymous environment, they can get the information they need on topics ranging from boys and porn to the facts about puberty. Amy gives her customers the information and skills to confidently talk with their kids and, in her words, "Make sex talks rock!"

7. Thank Them

This is by far the easiest thing you could possibly do, and yet people do it the least. What has happened to good old-fashioned thank-you notes? Just take a minute to write one, look up the address, grab a stamp, stick it in your mailbox, and you're good to go. Five minutes, max. Even saying "thanks" by e-mail works as an authentic way to connect with and appreciate customers. But these days it's rare. That's why I couldn't believe my eyes when I received a delicate, hand-written thank-you note from the Roosevelt Vision clinic. It was the first time I had ever been in, so up until that point, I had absolutely no loyalty to the clinic. But just a few appreciative words in that note from Dr. Kathy Yang-Williams made a huge difference. I still need to have my prescription filled, and her clinic sells frames, so you can be sure that's where I'm headed. Keep in mind the power that one little note can have to entice customers to come back again.

WORD-OF-MOUTH MARKETING

Hopefully one of these examples will give you an idea. And if not, I hope you'll take a close look at your strengths and tap into them to do more with your customers. Once you do, they'll be far more likely to be in that end stage of the relationship cycle and be ready to refer you to their network. You will have reached the sweet spot of marketing success:

word-of-mouth marketing. This is where your customers willingly become a virtual extension of your sales team.

A big mistake I see people make is not asking for more business! In our culture, admitting you need some help used to be seen as a sign of weakness. But those days are over. People respond to calls for help, and, thanks to social media tools, support is just a few clicks away. In order for this to work, you've got to do two things. The first is to make it easy for your customers to help. You need to remember that people are busy, bombarded, and often wary of unwanted communication at times—even your VIP customers. That's why it's so important to make your request as clear and as simple as possible.

An example of a business that does this well is a hip, urban fabric store called Stitches. I received an e-mail from the owner, Amy Ellsworth. She'd won a number of awards in the past for being the best fabric store in the region. Nominated once again, she had her fingers crossed her store would come out on top but knew that wasn't enough. She decided to e-mail her customers a simple request for help, and it said something along the lines of, "Hey friends, CitySearch is doing its annual 'Best Store' contest and we've been nominated. I really want to win this one. If you have already voted for us, thank you! If not, and you think we're a cool place, please consider placing your vote; the last day to vote is October 13th. Here's the link...." The short e-mail was easy to read, and by providing the link, she made the voting process straightforward. Amy has such a great store and is a fantastic business owner, who wouldn't want to help her? And guess what. She won!

So keep in mind, your customers are one of your greatest assets and strengths. Best of all, they are right at your fingertips, just waiting for you to give them some attention and deepen your connection. And if you play your cards right, they just might become part of your virtual sales team and tell the world how great you are. That's why when it comes to your marketing plan, you want to make sure your customers are front and center.

The Marketing Mindset

Take a few minutes to reflect on what you've read in this chapter and answer the following questions:

1. Do you need to find new customers or do more with the ones you have?

2. Referring back to the relationship cycle, where do you need to focus your efforts?

3. Do you know your VIP customers? Do you know where they are, what they care about, and how they want to connect with you?

4. What's in it for them to do business with you? What products and services can you offer that deliver extra value and benefit for them?

5. Is there a way your customers can help you?

CHAPTER 6

Form Powerful Partnerships

ONE THING SEATTLE IS known for is its coffee, but there's an innovative partnership happening around another "bean" in the city: the cocoa bean. The Chocolate Box is a retailer celebrating and selling goods from unique chocolatiers around the world. In addition to offering sipping chocolates and vegan sweets, the owners teamed up with some of Seattle's most famous chocolatiers to create a unique experience for customers called the Tour de Chocolat.

With The Chocolate Box at the wheel, chocoholics boarded a luxury van and began a cross-city tour of three different chocolate shops. The first stop was a chocolate factory tour at Theo Chocolates, the country's only bean-to-bar organic and fair trade chocolate factory. Next came a visit to Fran's Chocolates. The owner, Fran Bigelow, has been in the confectionery business for 30 years. Today, people around the world covet her candy, and President and Mrs. Obama are especially fond of her chocolate-covered salted caramels. The final stop was at Oh! Chocolate, where for more than 50 years, three generations of the Krautheim family have been crafting premium artisan chocolates. In between stops, tour participants enjoyed scenic views of Puget Sound and received educational stories and tips about chocolate. At the end of the tour, customers returned to The Chocolate Box for a final round of sampling and shopping.

Since its initial launch, The Chocolate Box has evolved the tour into what it now calls The Chocolate Box Experience. It still includes a factory tour of Theo Chocolates, but has added more educational and hands-on experiences for customers, such as making their own treats and watching chocolate in the making with some of the nation's most esteemed chocolatiers. The experience ends with a souvenir gift bag filled with samples from The Chocolate Box's own private label, custom chocolate bars, and discount coupons for shopping after the tour.

By working together, these four businesses were able to build upon their individual strengths and maximize their efforts to create a completely new experience for all of their customers. Instead of competing against one another, they collaborated to pool their marketing time, budget, and resources. The result? Since the tour began, The Chocolate Box has seen a tremendous increase in sales, received positive media coverage across the country, and has helped to put Seattle on the map as one of the hottest chocolate spots in the United States. "We got a tremendous amount of publicity from the original tour and it really launched us," says Michel Brotman, founder and master chocolatier at The Chocolate Box. "We've never spent a dime on marketing since then and we continue to get word of mouth and viral marketing from our customers about how much they enjoy the tour."

THE BENEFITS OF PARTNERING

Here's the situation. You've heard it before. Two brains are better than one. I'd take this a step further to say four arms can get a lot more done than two, and you'll reach many more people by combining mailing lists. There's a lot to get done when it comes to your marketing, so why not strengthen your efforts by teaming up to create something more powerful than you could ever do on your own.

I mentioned earlier how hard it is to break through all the noise and clutter to get your voice heard, e-mail read, Facebook page commented on, and so on. But if you team up with at least one other company, you improve your odds significantly. Your individual marketing messages become so much stronger when combined with other brands; they add a level of validation to your story—and more value for your customers. Not to mention that when you try to do all of your marketing activities on your own it can be time-consuming and expensive. From large corporations to solo-preneurs, when it comes to getting things done, two resources are often better than one.

But even though we know this to be true, forming powerful partnerships can be harder than we imagine. Some people are concerned that a potential partner will take advantage of the situation and even steal ideas, so they keep their cards held close to their chest, preventing any true partnership from ever forming. I've seen others do the opposite and give too much away when it comes to ideas, energy, and resources. A lot of women-owned small businesses do this and make a number of mistakes when they try to team up with another organization. They treat it as a friendship instead of as a marketing strategy. They meet at a networking event, hit it off, and the next thing you know, one of them is saying to the other, "Wouldn't it be fun if we did a workshop together?" Like speed dating, they rush into the first rendezvous without knowing much about the other on a personal level, let alone the brains behind her business.

Inevitably, one lets the other down by not holding up her end of the partnership. She is late to meetings, never gets around to writing the marketing plan as promised, or, as it turns out, doesn't have as large a mailing list as she had originally boasted. No matter the reason, there is a professional clash of styles. In the end, their event isn't as successful as it could have been.

This doesn't mean you shouldn't consider creating powerful alliances. It just means you need to be very selective about whom you decide to team up with on marketing activities. Don't let yourself fall for the first potential partner who comes your way. Hold out and be choosey. Being smart and strategic with your collaborative efforts can pay off. Remember, you have a lot of unique strengths to share and you want someone who can meet you halfway. And that's what this is really about; it's about finding an individual or organization able to complement what you have to offer. A partner to fill in the gaps, help smooth out your weaknesses, and round out your story.

PARTNERSHIP, ALLIANCE, OR COLLABORATIVE EFFORT

Right off the bat, I want to clarify what I mean by *partner* and some of the related terms I'll be using in this chapter. When I use the word *partner*, I'm referring to someone or some organization *outside* of your business. This is not someone you co-create your business with, and it's not a legally binding business arrangement. I'm talking about an informal collaborative effort; the action of teaming up to strengthen your story, maximize your resources, and help you get better results. This type of partner helps co-create and conduct a marketing activity with you, and in some cases, the responsibility, work, risks, and profits.

GUIDING LIGHTS NETWORK

One example of an organization that has built its brand around creating successful partnerships is The Guiding Lights Network, based in Seattle. The group specializes in the art of the gathering; creating experiences that spark civic imagination and social change. For more than seven years, the organization has brought together hundreds of leaders and change-makers from all across America to participate in the annual Guiding Lights weekend conference on creative citizenship. Packed with inspirational speakers, innovative ideas, and discussions, the weekend event is inspiring a movement to reimagine American citizenship and reclaim our democracy.

The most recent event, held at Seattle Center, sold out with more than 450 participants, and the Guiding Lights management team says it owes the movement's success to its collaborative efforts and to the incredible partnerships it has formed. Behind the scenes, this massive undertaking is managed by a small team of dedicated people: Eric Liu, Jená Cane, Claudette Evans, and Chris Ader, with event management by Alex Martin and Jubilee Event Engineers. But through this team's passion for creating professional relationships and alliances, it has strengthened its abilities and expanded its reach.

Building a diverse list of partners has been key to the event's success. The virtual Guiding Lights team includes a long and growing list of national and local luminaries, sponsors, attendees, community partners, staff, and volunteers who strive to live by the principle, "We're all better off when we're all better off!" And indeed, when everyone works together in mutual obligation to help ensure the success of the event, not only does it run smoothly, but it also delivers incredible value and an unforgettable experience for every participant.

⫸   ⫸   ⫸

These types of business alliances you form for mutual benefit may last for the duration of a short-term project or could evolve into a longer-term relationship. You collaborate with this person or business to produce something that benefits both your organizations. Call it what you want, but in this chapter, partnering is all about joining forces with another entity to move your business forward. It's about forming a strategic marketing partnership that pays off.

That's why these types of alliances are a smart move to consider as part of your marketing mix. They help you maximize your resources and grow more quickly and cost-effectively than you might on your own. You can leverage each other's unique strengths, extend your efforts, and do something amazing you couldn't do alone.

It's too bad that so many people in the traditional business world talk about competing with, clobbering, and even crushing the competition. These are such negative words. Just picture Coke and Pepsi, or Microsoft and Apple TV commercials, and you'll know what I mean. I've seen businesses be much more effective when they flip this stereotype around and instead start collaborating with their competitors and industry partners. A smart strategy for any marketing plan is to consider ways to partner with businesses that complement what you do. Remember the Guiding Lights' principle: "We're all better off when we're all better off!"

GREG KUCERA GALLERY

Despite lean times in the last few years, the Greg Kucera Gallery has never stopped growing in its 30 years of being in business. Greg says that with good fortune, hard work, and driving discipline, buying his retail space has turned out to be the best decision he ever made.

The gallery participated in its first art fair in 1985 and has been in more than 50 since then in cities such as New York, Miami, San Francisco, Los

Angeles, and Chicago. "We've tried to maintain a constant visibility over time and these activities keep us in the minds of collectors from around the country," says Greg.

Another marketing tool that helps the gallery gain exposure is its Website, regularly lauded as the most complete, user-friendly, and often-visited site of any gallery in the country. "I constantly hear from collectors that they check it all the time, using it comparatively with other galleries," says Greg. "It accounts for a great deal of our business and it also saves us time every day as a reference point for viewing our artists' work."

But Greg says one of the smartest moves he made for his business was helping to create the Seattle Art Dealers Association (SADA), which just enjoyed its 20th anniversary. Greg was a founding member and today serves as group president, helping to promote cultural and educational activities. Social media may have its time and place, but Greg says the continuity of galleries in the city is directly tied to a collaborative effort by the SADA to produce a monthly gallery guide. "The costs of participating are high, but the ease of getting it published each month and sent to a shared mailing list of 14,000 collectors makes up for the expense," says Greg. "We can illustrate something in the guide or on our Website and find it sold just by being the signal image for a show," says Greg. "It's very gratifying to create a response to a show before we even get the work installed." By combining efforts with other gallery owners, Greg is able to extend his marketing reach and move his gallery forward.

WHAT TO LOOK FOR IN A PARTNER

If you think this is an option for you, the first thing you need to do is set some criteria for what type of individual or organization would make the best partner. Here is a list of conditions to keep in mind.

1. Common Vision and Similar Goals

You've already done this work and are clear about your own future direction. Now you need to find a partner who shares your long-term goals. Maybe he or she wants to help improve the environment or educate families about domestic violence. If you have the same dreams, you just might make good partners.

And when you collaborate on a marketing activity, you'll have to set SMART objectives. If you're both in desperate need of more sales or trying to get more people to watch your YouTube videos, it might make sense to team up to get the results you both need.

2. Related Brand Attributes

What do you stand for? What story are you trying to tell? How do you want your customers to think and feel when they interact with your brand? If the qualities of your brand overlap with another business's characteristics, you may have a match made in heaven.

3. Shared Customer Segment

Have you come across another business that's also trying to reach divorced men in their 40s in corporate jobs who have custody of at least one kid and are amazing cooks? Then by all means explore the possibility of working together to create a combined message and joint stories that resonate with this niche audience you both need to reach.

ALASKA AIRLINES—FIRST FISH

The corporate culture of Alaska Airlines is deeply focused on creating relationships with its partners, large and small. In this story, you'll see how the company collaborated with a variety of organizations that all shared a common goal: creating a positive event for the community. By teaming up in this way and aligning their brands, they all got a business boost and dished up some fun for the public—literally.

Alaska Airlines plays a major role in supporting the state of Alaska's seafood industry, which is recognized worldwide for its sustainable fishing practices. In 2011, the carrier's cargo division delivered more than 23 million pounds of fresh Alaskan seafood throughout the United States, including nearly 700,000 pounds of Copper River salmon. For the past six years, this division of the airline has found an innovative way to acknowledge its valuable partners up north by hosting an annual celebration tied to the season's first catch of prized Copper River salmon.

"With roots in the state of Alaska spanning 80 years, we're proud to serve our customers and communities across the state from Sitka to Barrow and are especially honored to partner and support the Alaska seafood industry," says Torque Zubeck, managing director of Alaska Air Cargo.

The day begins early when a Boeing 737 is stocked in Cordova, Alaska, with about 24,000 pounds of fresh salmon from three seafood processor partners: Ocean Beauty Seafoods, Trident Seafoods, and Copper River Seafoods. The first shipment arrives at the Seattle-Tacoma International Airport's Alaska Air Cargo warehouse around 6:30 a.m. After the pilot opens the plane door and holds up the first ceremonial fish, the festivities begin.

Since 2010 the festivities have included a cook-off immediately after the fish arrives in Seattle. The 45-pound Copper River king salmon is filleted; local executive chefs start their grills and compete for the best salmon recipe in a "Copper Chef Cook-off." Each chef has just 30 minutes to prepare and serve the first catch of the season to a panel of judges who recently included Seattle Mariners Hall of Famer Jay Buhner, and Mike Fourtner, deckhand on the F/V Time Bandit, as featured on The Discovery Channel's *Deadliest Catch*.

The airline uses its marketing and PR resources to help promote all of its partners and build awareness for the event. Social media activities are also part of its marketing. The company uses its Twitter account, @AlaskaAir, to instantly announce the winning Copper River salmon recipe and to share all of the recipes prepared at the event. Fish lovers are encouraged to share their own favorite salmon recipes on Twitter, using the hashtag #CRsalmon. In addition, the airline has invited Facebook fans and select frequent fliers to participate as sous-chefs in the cook-off and win prizes.

"From the fisherman, the seafood processors, and those that work in the processing plant to the restaurants in the lower 48 states that serve the fresh seafood, the fishing industry is a huge economic driver for Alaska's communities and beyond," said Darbie Kirk, cargo marketing manager.

Although the cargo division of Alaska Airlines is relatively small in size compared to its passenger operation, this partner-focused marketing campaign is important to the company in that it deepens its partner relationships and builds overall goodwill toward the Alaska Airlines brand. The true return on investment is measured by the positive impact the program has for the community and everyone involved.

WHERE TO FIND PARTNERS

If you decide to pursue a partnership, how do you go about finding the right people and groups to partner with? Here are some different places to look and types of organizations to consider.

1. People in Your Industry

Similar to your customers, you probably have a handful or more of other businesses that interact with you on a regular basis. This could range from your graphic designer to the caterer for your lunch meetings. These are people you already know; businesses you're familiar with and organizations that have established a positive working relationship with you. These might be people worth looking to for a possible partnership.

At one time I worked with one of the largest printing companies in the state. Each year, it hosted an industry event with a panel of VP-level speakers from Fortune 500 companies, think tanks, and media outlets from across the country. From globalization to digitization, the event drew hundreds of attendees from printing companies throughout the region who wanted to learn about industry trends and changes impacting their industry. The company spearheading the event reached out to all of its business partners, including paper suppliers, copier companies, and ink distributors, inviting them to be sponsors of the event. These companies couldn't wait to sign a check, set up a booth, and do whatever it took to help make the event successful for everyone involved.

2. People in a Completely Different Industry from Yours

When I was in Windhoek, Namibia, my new colleagues at the U.S. State Department had the good foresight to suggest I try traditional African meals at two very different local restaurants. A talented entrepreneur named Twapewa Kadhikwa runs the Xwama Cultural Village and Restaurant. The business combines a craft shop with a restaurant to promote traditional artwork and cuisine in one of Windhoek's largest suburban settlements. Twapewa welcomed me into her spacious restaurant with its thatched roof, eye-catching stone walls, and sand floors. Dining spaces were separated by reeds and furnished with carved wooden tables and benches. I was treated to a traditional Namibian meal of wilted spinach, delicious oshiwambo chicken, and mahangu porridge, made of millet.

I also had the opportunity to meet with Rebekka Hidulika, the 20-something owner of another restaurant. Rebekka spent her early years working on a cruise liner, but decided to trade a life onboard for a life in the kitchen and opened Fusion. The menu is a gourmet collection of the finest-quality, freshest-prepared African fare accompanied by South African wines and other beverages, including a homemade Namibian ginger beer.

When Rebekka first opened her doors, business was a bit slow.[1] Fusion is somewhat off the beaten path, located in a converted residential space on a corner in a quiet neighborhood. In addition to word-of-mouth marketing from her customers, she relied on Facebook, blogging, flyers, and a mailing list to boost her business through marketing. But one thing that really helped her restaurant succeed was her partnership with local hotels, safari outlets, and even cruise lines. By teaming up with them, she has been able to offer their patrons a delicious, authentic, unforgettable African meal. In return, they feed her a steady stream of new customers. By extending their reach and collaborating with the active tourism industry in Namibia, both women have been able to move their businesses forward.

3. People Who Need Your Help

Some of the best examples of strategic partnerships come from social entrepreneurs: people who go into business to make a profit *and* a positive impact on the world around them. I had the good fortune to participate on a panel with one of them when I was in Kuala Lumpur, Malaysia.

Devan Singaram wanted to help marginalized communities improve their livelihoods by providing them access to a worldwide market via the Internet. He knew that in many cases, indigenous craft makers earned less than 10 percent of the final sales price for their products sold in the global market. That's why he and his cofounder, Mike Tee, created Elevyn, an online platform that connects community-based sellers to a socially conscious market. They wanted to help indigenous people create online stores that could then be set up and managed by the communities themselves. This was no easy task as the two trekked into jungles and rural villages carrying cameras and computers. They worked hard to help local artisans set up online shops by typing product descriptions, uploading images, and creating PayPal accounts to directly receive funding.

Today, Elevyn works closely with non-government organizations (NGOs) and partners with other groups to expand its services and empower disadvantaged communities by providing training and advisory services. Elevyn's administrative costs are kept low to ensure that more than 75 percent of every item's sales price goes straight into the producers' pocket. A portion of sales made through Elevyn's online store fund specific causes that support local communities, such as buying books for a community school.

4. People Who Do Almost Exactly What You Do

This is where your competitors come into play. There might be professionals in your field who are not threatened by you and who are interested in collaborating on a marketing activity. Piper Salogga of Piper Lauri Salogga Interiors and Sara Eizen of Nest are two talented interior designers located in the same city. After meeting, they realized they were on the same mission to promote sustainability within homes by educating people about their favorite green furnishings and decorating practices.

They decided to join forces and create an event called Sit + Sip where people could come grab a seat and a glass of wine and have fun learning about how to create a hip, "healthy" home within one's style and budget. They held their first event at a local home décor store. The two women brainstormed together to create an action plan and divide the workload. They shared ideas and e-mail lists to help promote the event and spread the word. The results were far better than they expected. They drew nearly 100 people and got positive media exposure—and it led to new clients for both of them. They decided to continue their collaboration for a number of years and the series of programs eventually was renamed ReDecor Revolution.

"Common values and goals made it easy to originally work together," says Piper. "Knowing, recognizing, and being honest about our strengths and weaknesses helped a bunch too—Sara took on most of the details and follow-through tasks, making sure we stayed on target and kept the ball in the air. I was better at the big-picture planning, sales, and marketing." She adds, "A lot of respect and laughter go a long way!"

Today the two entrepreneurs are busy running each of their successful businesses. They no longer invest time in collaborating, but took the essence of what they learned and used it to elevate their businesses to the next level. Piper is quick to say that working together was a great catalyst for both women to explore their belief in sustainability and creating beautiful spaces in long-lasting and meaningful ways. "We not only developed our businesses but a created a good friendship as well," says Piper. "I'm sure it was the perfect stepping-stone for each of us to move to what was next in our personal and business fulfillment!"

COLLABORATING WITH YOUR COMPETITION

This last example of Sara and Piper isn't easy for everyone to absorb. "Why would I team up with a business that is my direct competition?" you might ask. "Won't he or she steal my ideas and take advantage of the situation?" These are absolutely valid concerns and fears. Throughout the years, I've seen a few businesses struggle when their concepts are ripped off and their intellectual property is taken. Let me first say that if you have these concerns, you probably don't need to create this type of partnership. But if you do need this type of partnership, you also need to consult with a lawyer to draw up a non-disclosure agreement (NDA) or some other document to protect your business and ideas. I'm not advocating that you reveal all of your trade secrets to your competition. Instead, I'm suggesting that you explore possibilities to strengthen your activities with partnerships that feel right and make good business sense. If you feel confident you have something you can share and would benefit from teaming up, then do it. But if you have any reservations, don't. There are plenty of other marketing activities you can pursue.

If you do think you're ready to give partnering a try, there are a few steps to follow to ensure you create a winning, collaborative effort. Once you've picked the person or organization, here's what you need to do next.

Step 1. Start Brainstorming

You can do this over the phone, via Skype, or face to face over lunch. Go through your ideas to be sure you're on the same page. What could you do together that would help both of your organizations? Share your vision, goals, and thoughts about your target market and individual brands. Be sure everything lines up. If you already have an idea about what you want to do, share it and see how the other person might be able to build upon it.

Step 2. Use Your Strengths

The next thing you want to do is identify who has what assets and who is bringing what to the table. Mapping these details out early will help prevent potential resentments. Sometimes one party in a collaborative effort feels taken advantage of because he feels as though he invested more time or resources than the other partner. In some cases, one partner might contribute through actual man-hours, while another provides a physical location for an event. You want to ensure that the partnership is an equitable relationship and that no matter who is putting in what, no one feels as though she got the wrong end of the stick.

Step 3. Make a Plan

At some point you'll need to determine what needs to get done, along with who is doing what and by when. I'll talk about this in more detail in Part IV, but for right now, just capture your high-level thoughts about what it will take to get the right results from your joint venture so that it will be successful for everyone involved.

YOUNG SCIENTIFIC EXPLORERS

This method of partnering is exactly what Dr. Mohamed Yunus Yasin did when he helped create a new program called Young Scientific Explorers (YSE). Mohamed, a chemical engineer, came up with an idea to help children develop an interest in science, but knew he couldn't do it alone. Immediately after he wrote his proposal he began to identify a range of individuals and groups he'd need on his virtual team in order to see the idea come to life.

He started by approaching groups that might be interested in supporting his program, and, thanks to a friend working at an NGO, found his
first partner focused on education. The two then started talking to more
friends about the project to see if they would be interested in volunteering,
and managed to get four additional people to form a core team. The team
quickly produced a booklet containing about 10 science experiments for
kids, and it included a tour map of all the exhibits at the National Science
Centre in Kuala Lumpur, Malaysia. This was to be used as an early marketing tool and would eventually be given to all volunteers and participating
students. The group was now ready to approach schools that might take
part in a test pilot.

"There was lots of resistance at the beginning," says Mohamed. "To be
fair, teachers are overworked and did not want another 'thing' to do. But
we kept going. We approached headmasters [and] parent-teacher organizations, and we approached the primary students. We were looking for
champions to help run the program within the school. Once we even spoke
to the guy who runs the school cafeteria!" Finally, after much passion and
persuasion, Mohamed and his team managed to convince nine schools to
be part of the initial rollout of the program. In each case, a different internal "champion" would introduce and lead the YSE program within each
school.

The next step was to find a group of volunteers to visit the school and
serve as tour guides at the Science Centre. "This is always the most difficult
part, finding people who are willing to donate their time for your cause,"
says Mohamed. He knew going into the project that it could be challenging
to find volunteers, so he specifically designed the implementation phase to
have only four people visit a school at a time, and require only four guides
at the National Science Centre. "We targeted students who were on their
summer break and reached them by talking with all kind of groups who
work with young people, be it religious, sports, educational, etcetera," says
Mohamed. They finally managed to recruit about 20 students and started
training them. Although some dropped out, there were enough volunteers
to run the pilot.

Finally, the program was underway and Mohamed and his team successfully conducted the project in all nine schools, receiving extremely positive feedback from all participants. After the program had run its course,

the YSE team held press conferences, appreciation dinners for the volunteers, and seminars for teachers and parents to share the result of all their work with as many people as possible. "We regularly sent recap letters and progress reports directly to the schools, and this helped create even more interest in the project," says Mohamed. "Some schools began to approach us instead, asking for the project to be implemented at their schools." YSE continued for four more years and eventually included many more schools and more than 3,000 participating students.

The success of the project motivated Dr. Mohamed Yunus to write and implement two more related proposals. One, called "Science Fair for Young Children," is now in the sixth year. It recently conducted more than 260 school, state, and national science fairs. The number of participants to date totals roughly 200,000. "The development of this program has been a spiritual journey for me, as well as a science project," says Mohamed. "I now play an advisory role, and will slowly retire from this and move on to inspiring children (and myself) through soccer or something like that; I'm not sure yet. It is amazing what children can teach you. They can remind you of things you have forgotten."

⠀

Forming a partnership with another organization—or many, as in the case of Mohamed and his YSE program—can be a great way to boost your business. Partnerships allow you to build upon your strengths and align them with complementary assets someone else brings to the table. Partnership is like marriage: It allows you to share and build on "win-win" relationships. Why not explore this option as a way to minimize your costs and maximize your efforts? I encourage you to look for creative ways in which you can collaborate with others to move your organization one step further.

The Marketing Mindset

Take a few minutes to reflect on what you've read in this chapter and answer the following questions.

1. How could a partnership strengthen your marketing activities?

2. Are you currently doing business with an individual or organization that might be a good fit for a marketing partnership? If so, who is it?

3. If not, list a few people or groups you could research for a possible partnership with an individual or organization. Here are some categories to consider:

   ⮞ Within the same industry

   ⮞ Potential competitor

   ⮞ Completely different business

4. What elements of your marketing plan so far would be important for you to share with a potential partner?

   ⮞ Vision and goals

   ⮞ Situation, including opportunities and challenges

   ⮞ Brand attributes and guidelines

   ⮞ Customer segment and niche market information

5. What resources do you have that would add value for a potential partner? Go back to the strengths in your SWOT grid, if it's helpful.

   ⮞ Budget

   ⮞ Location

   ⮞ Staff time

   ⮞ Mailing list

   ⮞ VIP customers

   ⮞ Media contacts

   ⮞ Industry expertise

   ⮞ Social media followers

   ⮞ Other

CHAPTER 7

Amplify Through Media and Opinion Influencers

I USED TO START all of my PR workshops with this question: "How many of you want to be featured on the *Oprah Winfrey Show* someday?" Nearly every hand in the room went up, time after time. Because Oprah is no longer producing her TV talk show I've had to change my question a bit, but whether I swap out Oprah with *Ellen*, National Public Radio (NPR), *Wired* magazine, or *The Huffington Post*, the response is exactly the same: Just about everyone dreams of getting his or her name in the news.

And why not? The publicity you get from the mainstream media is always free, and if you do it right, completely positive. Whether you're in startup mode or your business has been around for years, adding media activities to your marketing mix can be a great way to help you reach your business goals. Media outlets can strengthen your efforts in helping you tell your story.

The mainstream media has gotten a bad rap lately. With so many national newspapers folding and more and more people watching TV online through sites such as Hulu.com, it begs the question: Is the mainstream media dead? No, it's not. Despite what you hear about the demise of the media, there are still a lot of outlets out there to give you your 15 minutes of fame—and more.

Did you know there are more than 20,000 magazines published in the United States alone, with new ones hitting newsstands every year?[1] Add to that about 1,000 daily newspapers. Yes, some metro papers are crumbling, but others are just launching. There are thousands of radio stations and TV stations, and I didn't even try to count the number of blogs and Websites. That's good news all around. Everyone has a chance to share his or her story with the media.

The challenge in working with the media isn't that there aren't enough outlets, it's that they're in the driver's seat. They control the message, not you. Unlike advertising, in which you pay to say exactly what you want to say, the media make the final call on what stories they will use and when they will run. In order to be successful with the media, you have to put yourself in their shoes.

Before we go too much further, let's clarify some common terms and get to the heart of exactly who and what I mean by *the media*. When it comes to the word *publicity*, I'm going to interchange it with *public relations* (PR) and *media relations*. To me, they all represent the process you use when you're interacting with the media. You do that to try to get a positive story told about your organization, and that's what this chapter is all about.

When I mention just *the media*, I'm referring to the mass media; that is, the broad range of individuals and organizations focused on communicating news and information. There are three main types of media outlets: print media, which include any paper or printed publication such as a newspaper or magazine; broadcast media such as TV and radio stations; and online and mobile media outlets ranging from Websites to social news apps for phones and tablets.

Today, many media outlets use a blended or multimedia approach to communicate their news. For example, in addition to producing live news reports, National Public Radio (NPR) also makes them available as podcasts, offers written transcripts of the stories along with photos or slide shows, posts excerpts on Facebook, and also tweets about them.

The types of people working in media outlets who create the stories you watch, read, and listen to are grouped under the broad category of *journalist* and include: reporters, photographers, producers, editors, publishers, and everyone in between. Most of these people studied English, communications, or journalism in school and take their work seriously.

Then there's a new batch of people popping up in this field called *citizen journalists*. They play an active and important role in the process of creating and sharing news and information, but they are not professional journalists. Consider the person who uses her cell phone to take a video of a car sliding down an icy hill and sends it to her local TV station. She could be considered a citizen journalist, but she isn't on the payroll. There are also examples of citizen journalists in places such as the Middle East who help report major events from their war-torn cities to media networks around the world. The unregulated nature of citizen journalism has been criticized by professional or "big J" journalists for being too subjective and amateurish, but like it or not, the "little js" serve a role in rounding out the media and are here to stay. Last but not least are the new or social media outlets. I'm talking about bloggers, podcasters, Tweeters, and Facebookers. These people are using new media tools to share information within their communities and beyond. They may or may not have experience as journalists. Some are citizens, some are citizen journalists, and some work for mainstream media outlets that use these tools too.

A DAY IN THE LIFE OF THE MEDIA

When it comes to the media, everyone wants to work with them, but few people take the time to figure out how they work. Let me just cut to the chase: Their jobs aren't easy. They work in aggressive industries and regularly face tight deadlines to produce multiple stories on any given day. There's a lot more competition, especially with citizen bloggers and podcasters. Media outlets are at risk every day when it comes to losing advertisers, subscribers, and audience numbers. Everyone is fighting for mindshare.

Many of them are multitasking themselves to death. Think you have it hard? They often have to submit multiple blog posts, tweets, photos, and/ or print or broadcast stories in a day, and each must be compelling, accurate, and not have a single typo or grammatical error.

On top of that, their technology is changing by the minute. I once knew a newspaper columnist who used to be responsible for writing three articles a week. He was a thorough researcher, a terrific writer, and his stories were some of the most popular in the paper. In the past few years, due to limited resources, his editor expanded the scope of his job to include producing a blog post and five to 10 tweets every a day. In addition to that, he was responsible for taking his own photos and creating short videos for every story—for no additional pay. He didn't feel he could continue to create compelling, accurate, quality news stories under those conditions so he ended up leaving his position.

My point in sharing this story is to demonstrate the pressure journalists are under. They are people, just like you and me. They have careers to build, bills to pay, families to feed, and vacations they'd like to take. If you keep these things in mind and treat them as you would any other professional, you'll have much better success in using them to help share your stories and information.

There are a lot of talented businesspeople out there with interesting stories to tell, but to get noticed by the media, you need to do more than just talk about your business; you have to do it in a clear, compelling, news-focused way. This is where most people get stuck. Extroverts tend to go overboard and end up bragging about their business. They write a news release with the headline, "We're the best in town," or send a reporter an e-mail with a long list of every feature in their product. Introverted types do just the opposite. They become paralyzed with fear at the mere thought of working with the media and end up saying nothing.

Other common issues that crop up for people when they think about interacting with the media include feeling unsure about what to say, and fear of being misquoted, coming across as bragging, or looking incompetent. All of these fears are normal. One way to get "unstuck" is to keep reminding yourself that reporters are people, just like you. Unless they work for the *National Enquirer*, their goal isn't to make you look bad; they want you both to succeed. If you keep the focus on how you can help them produce a good story, you'll be more successful in all of your media activities.

That's why it's so important to think of the media as real people, like you and me. When you get ready to contact one of them, instead of treating it as though it's a sales pitch, you should think about it more as having a conversation. If you focus more on how you can help the reporter get the information he or she needs and less on how you can sell your product or service, you'll be much more successful.

Here's an example of what I'm talking about. An organic floral design company got a phone message from a reporter asking for an interview. The business owner felt nervous and anxious about returning the reporter's call. Instead of calling the reporter back, the owner called me and we strategized about how best to handle the situation. We discussed how to treat the call as a conversation, so the business owner could move out of a reactive, "I'm afraid of being interviewed" mode and into more of an empowered, "I'm able to help the reporter" position. It worked beautifully. The phone interview went smoothly, with the business owner listening carefully and sharing her expertise and tips with the reporter. The experience resulted in a positive story for the business—and the journalist.

THE POWER OF PUBLICITY

Are you ready to move forward and start putting publicity to work for you? Before you get started, keep in mind that your publicity activities need to support your business goals. You can send out a lot of press releases but if they don't move your organization forward, what's the point? It all depends on the vision you have for your organization and your short-term marketing objectives. Here are just a few ways free PR can bring real value to your business and help you get to the next level.

➠ Positions you as an expert in your field

➠ Brings more customers to your door

➠ Generates hits to your Website

➠ Increases your visibility

➠ Boosts your sales

You're in the business of selling products and offering services. The media is in the business of delivering news. Convince them your business is newsworthy and there's a good chance they'll pay attention.

In order to come up with your news items, the first thing you have to do is start thinking like a journalist. The best way to do that is to start paying close attention to stories produced by the media outlets you want to reach: Listen to the radio; read a newspaper; subscribe to a magazine; check out a podcast. Before you start e-mailing press releases to producers or calling reporters, you need to know what news they cover to make sure your information is relevant. That way, you'll know exactly what news they're looking for and how they put their stories together. This will ensure you get the publicity results you want when your moment in the media spotlight arrives.

For a quick way to see a variety of news stories and headlines, walk into your local bookstore and buy a few copies of magazines or newspapers you'd like to see run your story idea. Let's say you want to share a business story with the media. Read that section of your local newspaper, check out your regional business journal, or skim national business publications such as *The Wall Street Journal, Fast Company,* or *Inc.* magazine. Of course, you can check out their Websites, too, but if print is your goal, get your hands on some real paper. Just do something that helps you get more information about the media you want to reach.

JUNEBUG WEDDINGS

In 2007, Junebug Weddings was an up-and-coming wedding resource site founded by three wedding photographers: Blair deLaubenfels, Christy Weber, and Kim Bamberg. The site was rapidly becoming an innovative go-to resource for anyone needing to plan a wedding, but the founders needed to build more awareness to woo advertisers and subscribers. They thought media coverage could help with their goals, so they started to pay more attention to the local media outlets and the stories they were covering.

After brainstorming about possible news angles, they realized they had a creative, emotional, and statistical story to tell. The Junebug trio noticed that more and more of the professionals they worked with, from caterers to florists, were adopting eco-friendly practices. This was back before "going green" was as popular as it is today. As experts in their field, they spotted the trend and wanted to ensure green wedding planning would become an industry norm.

They pitched this story to their local media and ended up being interviewed for a series about "Living the Green Life" on 710 KIRO News Radio. Then the local business journal picked up their story, followed by regional magazines and TV shows. Today, Junebug is regularly featured in national media outlets and is one of the most popular, trend-setting, and well-respected wedding brands in the world.

WHAT MAKES SOMETHING NEWSWORTHY?

After you've done some sleuthing about the media outlet you want to reach and its reporting style, then you can get back to focusing on you and your news story. The mistake many people make in thinking about the news they have to share is coming up with ideas such as "we're the best business in town" and "our Website is the most popular." Maybe you are the best and the most popular. That's great. But the media isn't looking for those types of stories.

News in the media's mind is more topical or noteworthy information, often related to recent or important events. A news story includes specific facts and data to back up what you're saying. It's not about making claims of greatness; it's about sharing stories of interest. Think about it: News can be anything from a new movie theater opening in town to a nonprofit focused on helping teen girls produce video games. Maybe you do have the best milk-shakes in town. A good reporter would want to see your revenue numbers, talk to your customers, and maybe even check out your competitors to ensure your claim is actually true and worthy of a story.

Your business is one of a kind, so there's always an original story you can tell. You need to determine your news. This is where all of the work you've done so far can help. If you go back and look at your strengths and opportunities, your brand attributes, and stories about your customers and partners, you are bound to have something to share with the media. And planning ahead pays off. You want to map out your news ideas in advance to determine which are the best and strongest. That way you'll be more successful in attracting the media's eyes and ears.

Reporters use a variety of methods to come up with a good story. They follow trends, pay attention to current events, investigate issues that interest their audience, and often go with what their gut sense tells them is a story. To help you think like a reporter, here are three different types of news stories for you to consider: sensational, emotional, and statistical. After reading through the examples, you'll get a sense of how they work and how they might relate to your organization. You can use any if they help you talk about your business in a newsworthy way with the media.

1. Sensational

Media outlets always like a juicy story. Something controversial and shocking is guaranteed to be a good hook. If your business is doing something groundbreaking, the media will want to know about it.

If you can't think of something unique that you're doing in your organization, you can always look for ways to create something that's exciting news and thus newsworthy. There are awards you can apply for and contests you can enter. You could consider holding a publicity stunt. Or think about revealing a best-kept secret about your business—and then let the media in on it.

Before you head down this new path, you'll want to be sure you can answer questions similar to this:

➠ What are you doing that's amazing and extraordinary?

➠ What makes your story so provocative and fascinating?

➠ Has your business received recognition from a notable or celebrity source?

To get you thinking, here are three real-world "sensational" sample headlines:

➠ "First 'ski-thru' Starbucks now open"

➠ "Spectacular Irish hotel, massive discount price"

➠ "Expert says loyalty programs are a waste of money"

2. Emotional

It doesn't matter if it's about senior citizens, puppies, or single mothers, the media love to tell stories that tug on our heartstrings. That's why sharing the human or emotional side of an issue related to your business can make a powerful news hook. From radio interviews to online magazine articles, many media outlets share expressive and poignant stories with the public. To make your human-interest story more compelling for the media, let them know if you have photos or videos that can help convey the feeling behind the story. You can create this content by hiring a professional photographer or videographer, or even asking a friend or intern to help you.

To determine if this style of story is a good fit for your business, here are some questions to answer:

➠ Does your organization work to solve an important social issue?

➠ Do you have a powerful customer story or testimonial you can share?

➠ Are you doing something that makes people happy and improves their lives?

To get you thinking, here are three real-world emotional sample headlines:

➠ "Yoga saved my life: one man's story"

➠ "Piano store brings Mozart to disadvantaged youth"

➠ "Soldier shows love 6,000 miles away with organic flowers"

3. Statistical

Media outlets love numbers! Take a close look at the cover of any popular outlet and you'll see headlines about the top 10 ways to do X or the five reasons you need Y. Chances are you've already done a lot of research about your topic and have interesting data right at your fingertips. If you have some interesting numbers to back up your story, share that information with the media.

One way to create some interesting statistics related to your news topic is to use an online survey tool such as Surveymonkey.com. It can help you quickly gather and analyze information from people around the world on any topic—for free. Or invite a group of your customers to talk about a subject with you and share the results with the media. Voila! You have news!

To determine if a statistical story is a good fit for your business, here are some questions to answer before you get started:

➠ Can you come up with a Top 10 Tips list?

➠ What numbers do you have access to about your industry?

➠ Can you debunk three common myths about your business?

Here are three real-world statistical headlines to get you thinking:

➠ "7 ways to shop smarter"

➠ "Gallery shares six tips for art collectors"

➠ "Survey shows sleep may improve with age"

HOW TO MAKE YOUR PITCH

Once you've brainstormed and come up with a list of news ideas, the next thing you need to do is start creating your pitch. In baseball, when the pitcher tosses a ball toward home base, the batter only swings if he thinks it's a good throw and has a chance of hitting it. And if he hits it out of the park and gets a home run, fantastic! This is similar to what you're doing. You're tossing your news idea to a reporter and hoping he or she likes it enough to take a swing.

Basically your pitch is like an elevator speech: a short, compelling story you share with the media in an e-mail, over the phone, or in a concise press release. Remember, they're busy, on deadlines, and working in a competitive environment. You've got to capture the media's attention quickly, so you've got to make your pitch powerful. The best way to learn how to do this is to go back to the media outlets you've been researching. Take a close look at the first paragraph in an article or listen to the first few sentences of a radio news story. Whether it's a review of a new restaurant or an interview with an author, all good media stories grab your attention in a matter of minutes with just a few words, sounds, or pictures.

Another thing you'll notice in most media coverage is that the first few lines of a story or the first few minutes in a broadcast news report are usually a summary. It's standard for them to touch on these six elements of the story: who, what, when, where, why, and how. If you include these things in the start of your pitch, you'll up your odds of hooking the attention of a reporter. It's all about telling your story in the most effective, compact, and compelling way possible.

You begin by writing a headline or a condensed version of your news in one sentence. This is especially helpful to do because you can repurpose it as the subject line in an e-mail pitch. You want to write it exactly as you'd like it to be read, seen, or heard in the media.

The goal is to make it as easy as possible for the media to use your pitch. Some small outlets or those with limited resources might even use exactly what you write, especially if it's written in their style of storytelling and conveys the news in an objective, engaging way. So start yours out with a bang.

Here's an example of an actual news release used as a pitch by documentary filmmaker Wyatt Bardouille. It's one that worked well to hook the media and instantly got attention:

FOR IMMEDIATE RELEASE

Media contact: Wyatt Bardouille

wyatt@bardouille.com

1-425-922-5311 (USA)

Documentary about Dominica as a Sustainable Nation Screens at Film Festival in Barbados

Seattle, WA—February 14, 2012. Dominican-American filmmaker Wyatt Bardouille, along with her mother and sister, returned to Dominica in 2008 to make a film about her roots. Together, the women uncovered a much deeper story about the island and its history of devastating hurricanes, political upheaval and limited resources. The new documentary, *Dominica: Charting a Future for Paradise*, tells the story of how the Nature Island nation faces challenges in its continuing struggle for development in a competitive, global world. The film was just accepted into the Africa World Documentary Film Festival and will be screened at the University of the West Indies, EBCCI Cinematheque from March 8 to March 11, 2012. Please visit *www.africaworldfilmfestival.com* for exact date, time and ticket availability.

"This engaging 35-minute feature with powerful voices, striking visuals and iconic music, tells the Dominica story through those who have lived it," said Mervin Matthew of GIS News, Dominica.

Like Barbados, Dominica is expanding from an economy based primarily on agriculture to one tapping the other gifts that nature has bestowed upon it. The film tells the remarkable story of how Dominicans, both local and abroad, are coming together to develop the "future industries" of ecotourism and green energy, and move agriculture in a more sustainable direction. It captures the essence of the island and its culture with brilliant imagery and evocative island music.

About the Film and Filmmakers

More information, including a film trailer, film synopses, a director's statement, credits and production photos, can be found at the Website *www.dominicaparadisefilm.com*.

About the Africa World Documentary Film Festival

The Africa World Documentary Film Festival (AWDFF) is sponsored by the E. Desmond Lee Professorship in African/African American Studies, Center for International Studies, University of Missouri–St. Louis. AWDFF has been bringing fascinating stories of Africa and the African diaspora to all corners of the globe since 2007. For more information visit the Website *www.africaworldfilmfestival.com*.

About Bardouille Productions

Bardouille Productions is an independent film production company which also specializes in Web-based media production. It produces narrative and documentary films as well as entertaining and informative content for the Web. The company implements all aspects of production, both creative and technical, to craft provocative, engaging subject matter and programming. More information can be found at the Website *www.bardouille.com*.

This release worked so well, it was picked up verbatim by the *Bajan Reporter*, one of the top sources for breaking news in Barbados and throughout the Caribbean. To date, Wyatt has received media coverage in TV, radio, and online outlets around the world.

⫸   ⫸   ⫸

You now know how to come up with news ideas that will grab the media's attention. Once you've written out your most compelling pitch, all you have left to do is package up your story and get it to the right reporter, producer, or editor. Most media outlets are open to you contacting them in a variety of ways. Most have a "send us your news" section on their Website. You can also pick up the phone and call their reception desk and ask. Respect their guidelines and do what they say. If they ask you to e-mail them your release, do it. If they want you to upload a short news pitch onto a Web form, do that. Follow their lead.

From e-mailing a news release to hiring a PR consultant to help you, it's up to you to decide how much time and money you want to invest and how comfortable you are doing your own publicity. The sooner you give one of these methods a try, the sooner you'll be on your way to knowing what works best for you and your business!

My advice is to focus on your strengths. If you're an introvert, or you love to write, you might prefer to send an e-mail. If you're an extrovert, have an engaging voice, or love to talk, make a phone call. You can also invite a reporter to meet you for coffee to discuss issues impacting your business or industry.

USING NEWSWIRE SERVICES

In most cases, publicity is free. If you do the outreach to the media yourself, using e-mail, the phone, or even snail mail, it doesn't cost you a thing but your time (and maybe some postage). But in some cases, it makes sense to get a little help, especially if you need to reach a lot of reporters quickly. A great way to do that is to use what's called a wire service. These organizations are in the business of supplying news stories to media outlets. They can instantly deliver your news straight to credentialed journalists, bloggers, and key influencers all over the world. All large corporations use these services to distribute their press releases, and they are accessible and affordable for small businesses too.

There are a number of these services, ranging from PR Newswire, which pioneered the commercial news distribution industry nearly 60 years ago, to tools such as PRWeb, which also help your news get found fast, and first. I've used many of them, but have worked with PR Newswire most frequently and have seen the powerful results a wire service can deliver. I first utilized PR Newswire when I worked at Microsoft and have since used their services when working with smaller businesses.

For PR Newswire members, the process is remarkably simple. With just a few clicks, you can upload your news story, choose a distribution circuit, add a photo or other multimedia element, and select your distribution date and time, and your news is released to the world. PR Newswire has the ability to send your information to more than 60,000 news and social media outlets. You can reach almost all of the sports reporters on the West Coast or fashion bloggers around the world. For just a few hundred dollars, a small business can have its news distributed globally in minutes. In addition, they'll provide you with detailed analytics that let you see the immediate impact of your news online. You'll learn how many people read your release, where it was picked up, and how many times it was shared.

Rachel Meranus, vice president of marketing and communications at PR Newswire, shares her insight into the evolution of the wire service industry: "'Wire service' is a misnomer," she says. "We enable organizations of all sizes to create, optimize, target, and distribute all types of content (text, multimedia, photos, compliance-related documents, and more) across all channels (traditional, social, search, Web, and mobile), and monitor and measure the results of those efforts."

One growing trend she's noticing right now is how many organizations are adding multimedia components to their press releases. "Not only does it give you more chances to be seen due to the sheer fact that you have more assets to distribute across different channels, but studies show that when a press release includes multimedia elements, the level of engagement with the content increases by 77 percent."

In addition, she's seeing stories and information being accessed by more than just the media. "A business will send out a press release and link to a white paper or a Webinar signup page. Press releases are leading readers directly to a transactional opportunity—such as buying a product online or donating to a cause. They are truly becoming digital marketing tools."

THE SNOWBALL EFFECT

Publicity has an amazing snowball effect. Once you start getting coverage, you begin attracting the eyes and ears of more journalists. As I mentioned, it's a competitive business so they watch each other carefully to see who is covering what. As a result, you never can predict where your PR efforts will take you. Elisabeth Dale is a perfect example of this. She's the author of a book called *bOObs: A Guide to Your Girls*, which is all about educating and empowering women about their breasts.

While researching her book, Elisabeth facilitated breast health workshops for teen girls, and she worked with a boutique PR agency to pitch the news to the media. A local newspaper found the talks intriguing and sent a reporter and photographer to cover the story. The result was a massive cover article including a color photo of Elisabeth in action. A regional TV show saw the story and interviewed her, too. The next thing you know, she was getting a call from a producer at *Good Morning America* in New York. After her interview on that national talk show, Elisabeth was invited to write a column for the *London Times*. Today she's built her business into an online empire called TheBreastLife.com and is regularly contacted by national and international media such as *Glamour*, *Women's Health*, and *Cosmopolitan* to comment and share her expertise on everything from breast cancer to sports bras. And it all started with one story.

⇒   ⇒   ⇒

Working with the media is a great way to move your business forward. When you do publicity right, media outlets can serve as virtual extensions of your team and help you strengthen your marketing activities. I encourage you to take a look at your business and determine what news stories you might have at your fingertips. Sensational, emotional, or statistical, you probably have a range of news to share that would make great stories. Consider pursuing publicity as a way to maximize your marketing—for free.

The Marketing Mindset

Take a few minutes to reflect on what you've read in this chapter and answer the following questions.

1. What are your specific publicity goals?
   ➠ Bring more customers to your door or Website
   ➠ Distinguish you from the competition
   ➠ Position you as an expert in your field
   ➠ Generate sales and revenue
   ➠ Increase your visibility
   ➠ Other

2. Which types of media outlets can best support your business through free publicity?
   ➠ Print
   ➠ Broadcast
   ➠ Online
   ➠ Combination

3. Take a crack at writing your own sensational, emotional, or statistical news hook. Start with the idea that best fits your business. Write your one-sentence headline.

4. Go a step further. What story do you want to tell? What else can you say that will hook a reporter in the first few seconds? Write the first paragraph of your news pitch as though you were a reporter covering the story. Use the following key elements to help you.
   ➠ Who
   ➠ What
   ➠ When
   ➠ Where
   ➠ Why
   ➠ How

5. Which method would work best for you to contact the media?

    ➠ Send an e-mail.

    ➠ Make a phone call.

    ➠ Distribute a press release using a wire service.

    ➠ Hire a PR consultant to coach you.

    ➠ Submit your news via an online form on their site.

PART IV

SIMPLICITY:
Keep the Plan and Process Straightforward

The secret of getting ahead is getting started. The secret of getting started is breaking your complex overwhelming tasks into small manageable tasks, and then starting on the first one.
—Mark Twain

Whether you've read through the entire book sequentially and reflected upon your marketing strategy, story, and strengths, or you've jumped straight to this section, I'll assume your mind is buzzing with ideas on how to get started creating your marketing plan. You have clear goals, a good amount of research to back you up, and many projects you want to implement. On paper, and especially in your head, it's a maze of information that begs to be simplified. And that's the theme of this section: simplicity.

The following two chapters will help you identify your resources (so they're used in the most efficient way possible) and formulate and complete your action plan.

In Chapter 8, you'll learn how to turn all the marketing ideas you've pulled together so far into an effective action plan. I'll show you how to keep it simple and focused on the most important elements of what needs to get done, who needs to do it, and by when. You'll find that once you have your plan mapped out, it's much easier to take those first steps toward success.

In Chapter 9, you'll find many ideas for aligning your resources to avoid duplicating effort and wasting money and time. Through case studies, you'll learn how several businesses started with almost nothing, but grew significantly by maximizing their greatest assets and taking advantage of simple tools right at their fingertips. You'll also see how some global corporations used the same methods to pounce on opportunities as they arose.

Keeping things simple starts with streamlining your efforts and leveraging the resources you already have at your disposal. From there, you can easily produce a straightforward planning document that keeps your marketing on track and your projects doable so you can continue down the path of forward-moving progress.

CHAPTER 8

Create an Action Plan

So far I've discussed the principles of strategy, story, and strengths, and used them to help you define your vision and goals, build your brand and story, and identify who can help boost your efforts. Now I'm going to show you how to turn all of the valuable information you've gathered so far into a streamlined action plan. By putting the most important details in one place, you'll be able to more easily manage all of your marketing activities. I should point out that, although marketing is an essential *part* of your overall business plan, it is helpful to pull it out into its own, separate document. That's what I'm going to help you create: a simple, stand-alone planning tool to help you move forward with your marketing.

This plan takes into consideration everything we've built upon in the book, going back to the original vision, mission, goals, and objectives—all the ideas you've gathered so far. At this point, you might think you're going to create a campaign that involves forging new partnerships, or that you may need to build a VIP customer program. Whatever you've decided you need, you should now create something to help consolidate the project information, clarify the details, and get it into one place where you can easily stay on top of everything that needs to get done. Your action plan is that place where everyone (you and your team, your partners, your investors) can come together on one page—or in one place—and work together to use marketing to help you reach the next level. Once you have your plan in hand, you can turn it into real action.

GET HITCHED GIVE HOPE

One organization that greatly benefited from putting a simple marketing plan in place is Get Hitched Get Hope (GHGH), a nonprofit organization with a unique twist: It holds an annual auction of wedding goods and services to raise money to grant wishes for terminally ill patients. In other words, it's a huge, swanky party for brides and grooms who want a fun way to shop for everything from flower arrangements to vacation packages—and make a difference at the same time.

With the help of a bottle of wine, a group of six wedding professionals came up with the idea for GHGH at a monthly networking event. They told each other, "Wouldn't it be great if we could create an event that would bring members of the local wedding industry together *and* raise money for a great cause?" Coming up with the vision was the easy part. The group had a lofty goal of throwing an event that would raise $50,000 for a charity, but they weren't sure how they were going to do it.

"We ended up working backwards," says Barbie Hull, a seasoned wedding photographer and one of the group's founders. "We started by picturing the end result, seeing our idea of a huge, successful party, and from there, we worked our way back and figured out everything that needed to be done to get us there."

In the early days of planning, the group had a long to-do list to tackle. Everything from creating a Website and writing press releases to finding the right location and securing sponsors and vendors. It was no easy task, as all of the founding members had full-time jobs and managed GHGH on a strictly volunteer basis.

When it came to getting all of the work done, Barbie says the group based everything on individual personalities. "We all talked about what our core values and strengths were and realized we each brought something different to the event-planning process," she explains. "Another gal and I were the vocal ones on the committee, so we were the obvious choices for PR. Another member was an awesome designer, so she was assigned marketing materials. A few other gals were professional event planners and were really strategic and serious, so it made sense that they focus on procurement. And then one girl, she had a vision, and her background was accounting and invitation-making, so she had both sides of her brain working, so she was the boss lady! She was our president and oversaw everything."

During the first year, the group decided not to use a marketing action plan. The ideas were flowing and things were happening so fast that taking time to create a plan felt like an unnecessary step. At the time, it seemed as though it might even slow down their progress. They didn't realize a plan would've made things much easier. "In that first year, it seemed like there were 100 million e-mails going back and forth between all of us and it was hard to stay on track," says Barbie. "The event was amazing and a huge success, but we ended up not hitting our specific fundraising goal."

But the group didn't give up.

"After the first event, we learned a lot. We ended up doing sort of a SWOT analysis at the end where we talked about what was realistic and what we'd need to be more successful when we did it again. We had each worked so hard and had treated it like a second job for an entire year, and we were disappointed we only raised $24,000. We knew we could do better, especially if we got a plan in place."

The group brainstormed how they could improve the event and make it more manageable for everyone involved. They acknowledged that GHGH needed a better way to organize its efforts, manage all of its volunteers, and stay on task.

"Our second year, we wrote a business plan, including an organizational chart, and it made a huge difference and helped us be much more efficient with our time. Every year the event got better and better, and by year three, we beat our goal!" says Barbie.

Today, GHGH has more than 30 people on its planning team, more than 100 sponsors, and an endless list of people who want to volunteer to support the cause.

"We're now in year five and I have no doubt we're going to raise $100,000 to give to The Dream Foundation," Barbie says. "We would never have come this far and been this successful if we hadn't taken that step forward regarding planning."

There are some basic elements to consider when getting started with your marketing plan. You need to know what needs to get done, who's doing the work, and when the tasks need to be completed. As simple as this seems, many individuals and organizations hold off on creating these helpful documents for various reasons. In the case of the smart, busy founders of GHGH, they were working on such a fun, exciting new project that in comparison, creating an action plan seemed to be boring and a waste of time—who can afford to sit around and plan when there are more important things to do? They ended up randomly doing activities that popped up but didn't matter in the long run and did not lead toward that original vision and goal. You can learn from their mistakes. If you want to grow organically, that's fine, but if you want to move forward at a faster pace and get the right results, you need to have a plan in hand.

THE FIVE STEPS OF AN ACTION PLAN

People on the other end of the spectrum from the seasoned professionals planning GHGH get overwhelmed at just the thought of having to come up with a marketing plan. They think it's going to be a very complicated process, requiring them to produce a long document with lots of spreadsheets—and it can be. I've worked in some organizations where people do convolute things, spreading the planning out for months and months, and in one case, ending up with a planning document made up of more than 100 PowerPoint slides.

It happens in smaller organizations, too. I once heard from a colleague who had decided to hire a marketing agency to help him launch his new business. "Whitney," he said, "would you take a look at this document? An outside consultant sent me this marketing plan and it's the most complex thing I've ever seen, with a $100,000 price tag attached to it. It doesn't make sense to me."

A plan might be filled with the best ideas and projects in the world, but if you can't read it, you can't use it, and if you can't use it, it won't help you move forward. The good news is that it doesn't have to be this way. An effective action plan for your marketing should be simple to create and easy to use.

As I mentioned at the beginning of this chapter, the best way to streamline marketing is to build upon the vision, goals, and SMART objectives you originally set. Remember the scorecard I introduced back in Chapter 1, the grid you created that showed your strategic direction? If you can stay focused on the core things most important to your business, your marketing will be much more effective. That's why I often advise people who want to be more successful with their marketing to start with the end in mind and work backward. Beyond just mapping out what success looks like, an equally important step is determining exactly how you'll get there. That's exactly what the GHGH leaders did in year two of their event planning. Having a simple action plan in place helped them move the event forward.

Creating a straightforward blueprint for what needs to get done is as easy as capturing a few details, including some basic metrics, and adding a level of accountability around what you're trying to accomplish. For example, you might have "Need to produce a digital brochure" on your marketing to-do list, but it never gets done. Without a defined owner, a specific approach, and a clear deadline, it's easy for a task such as this to stay on that list for a long, long time. To manage marketing projects well, you need a method to the madness, some type of simple system to keep track of all the details surrounding each activity.

So how do you get started figuring out what needs to be included in your plan? There are five basic steps:

1. Pick the project.
2. Define the categories.
3. Choose the planning tool.
4. Create the plan.
5. Use the plan.

This simple approach to thinking about your marketing works for small projects such as tweeting on Twitter, and for large-scale undertakings such as planning the GHGH event. I'm going to use a piece of direct mail, a postcard from Gold's Gym, as an example to show you how easy it can be to create an action plan to get something similar done in your organization.

Step 1. Pick the Project

In this first part of the planning process, you need to identify the marketing project you need to tackle. What tasks need to get done? This is all about breaking down your ideas into smaller pieces so you can better manage them. For example, in the case of Gold's, the project is to conduct a direct mail campaign to local customers. To get that project finished successfully, multiple tasks need to be completed, from designing the card to mailing it. Right now, all you need to do is think through all of the things that need to get done in order to get that postcard into people's mailboxes. Make a list of the tasks, ordered from largest to smallest or in chronological order. It doesn't matter what technique you use, just don't miss a piece of what it will take to complete the project. Here's a suggestion of how the first part of your plan might look:

Project: Direct Mail Campaign
Create postcard design
Write copy/text for card
Get stock photos
Get bids from printers
Get bids from mail house
Prepare mailing address database
Mail to customers

Step 2. Define the Categories

Now you move on to making sure you have the right categories in your plan so you can track the most essential things. This will give you the information you need to make sure your activities stay on course. Remember to keep things simple. If you use too many categories you could easily spend the majority of your time managing the plan and not make progress on your marketing. Following are five suggested categories.

1. Owner: Who is doing the work? Is it you? Are you delegating it to someone on your team? Do you need to outsource the task to a graphic designer or use an intern to help you?

2. Method: Where and how is the task going to get done? Are you sending a press release out using a wire service, or using your business e-mail account? Are you using WordPress to post to your blog or do you use a Web developer? In the case of Gold's, are you using an external mail house?

3. Budget: What's the cost? Is there a fee associated with the task? If so, how much? If you have multiple accounts, specify which budget line this activity will hit. This is a good time to be sure you have the budget needed to complete the task, too. To produce a post card, your costs could include everything from design and printing to securing stock photos and paying for postage.

4. Deadline: By when? What's the cut-off date or milestone for the work to be done? Are you completing all of these tasks in a day, or will it take you a month from start to finish to get this post card from the printer and into mailboxes?

5. Results: How will you know if you're successful? What will you do to measure and evaluate the marketing project? I will spend more time discussing metrics for success in Chapter 10, so for right now, refer back to your SMART objectives and use them.

Step 3. Choose the Planning Tool

This next step is about selecting the planning tool that works best for you. It needs to be a tool that allows you to consolidate all task-related information and makes it accessible to everyone involved. Remember, it doesn't have to be complicated. Some tools are simple, one-page documents with tables or lists of bullet points. Other tools that work well, especially for people who are more visual, are mind-mapping diagrams or pictorial representations of what needs to be done.

Here are a few suggestions of tools you might want to consider, from extremely simple to somewhat sophisticated. I've used them all for one project or another and they all have their place, depending on the project. It doesn't matter whether you're making blog posts or sending out a press release around the world—any of these could help you succeed. Pick a tool you think you'll use, and if it isn't working, try another approach to creating your marketing action plan.

Word or Excel: Your action plan can be as simple as a table inserted into a Word document or an Excel spreadsheet. It may not take much more than a few columns and rows to track the most important information about your marketing project.

Calendar: Some people use a simple calendar to keep track of what needs to get done, who is doing it, and when things are due. If that straightforward approach would work for you, use it.

1,2,3 Marketing Mechanism Calendar: Erica Mills of Claxon helps mission-minded nonprofit organizations do good and get noticed. After spending years helping everyone from the largest foundation on the planet to local food banks, she developed a very simple planning calendar as part of her 1,2,3 Marketing Tree approach. To keep your marketing low-stress and high-impact, she advises you pick just three activities to focus on. Here's an example of what her calendar looks like:

Mechanism	Budget	Success Metrics	Tasks	Due Date	Responsibility
Priority 1: Fliers	- 2 hours to create - 2 hours to post - $50 to print	- # of calls/ e-mails mentioning fliers - # of new clients from fliers	1. Create flier 2. Get it printed 3. Post flier	Jan 31 Feb 5 Feb 15	Sue Pat Pat
Priority 2					
Priority 3					

Google Docs: This tool is a great, free way to create a plan, share it with your team, and manage your progress. It only takes a few minutes to get everyone using and editing the same document in real time. Barbie from GHGH said they started using Google Docs in the second year, as part of their planning process, and it made all the difference in the world.

Project Bubble: This easy-to-use, online project management tool includes the ability to track details such as time spent on a project and allows for collaboration, progress reporting, and even creating an invoice. Projects can be created in a matter of seconds and then assigned to the people responsible for completing the task, along with a due date.

Basecamp: Task management is very straightforward with this online tool. In addition to the basics, it has a visual timeline of project activities that gives you surprisingly deep insight into who's working on what and what is getting done. It also has a nice dashboard feature that lets you see all of your activities and statuses on projects at a glance.

Microsoft Project: For larger marketing campaigns, such as global product launches with hundreds of team members and millions of budget dollars, this can be a very effective tool. One of its features gives managers a simple way of visualizing the sequence of tasks to prevent overloading an individual in the planning stages and quickly transferring assignments based on a person's actual time availability.

Step 4. Create the Plan

Once you've chosen the tool that's right for you, start filling in the blanks. In the case of the Gold's example I used earlier, here's what it might look like if I used a table in Word or an Excel spreadsheet to get the plan started:

Marketing Project	Owner	Method	Budget	Deadline	Results
Create postcard design	Pam	Outsource to designer	$500	June 1st	Design complete
Write copy/ text for card	Barb	Word	N/A	June 8th	Copy written

Get stock photos	Barb	Istockphoto.com	$100	June 8th	Photos obtained
Get bids from printers	Pam	Call/Email	$1,000	June 15th	Bids received
Get bids from mail house	Pam	Call/Email	$750	June 15th	Bids received
Prepare mailing address database	Barb	Salesforce.com	N/A	June 22nd	Addresses finalized
Mail to customers	Pam	Use mail house	N/A	June 29th	Cards printed and mailed

Step 5. Use the Plan

With your plan in place, you're ready to start putting it to work for you. In order to do this, you need to decide how often you're going to use it. When will you check the plan and review what's getting done, and especially manage and monitor those deadlines to ensure you stay on track? Some people tackle their marketing activities on a daily basis, others monitor it weekly, and one accounting firm I know keeps marketing to a minimum and focuses on reviewing the plan every quarter. The way you use your plan will depend heavily on the overall rhythm of your business as well as the deadlines for your projects. What you want to avoid is creating a plan and then saving it on your computer or within Google Docs and never touching it again. Any plan you create is only valuable if it is a working tool that you actively use to help you succeed.

Tracking is one thing, but how often will you review your action plan to see if it's still valid? At a minimum, I'd suggest you review it every quarter to make sure it works well to support your business and marketing goals.

Remember that things within your plan will change. They always do. Your projects may change, deadlines can shift, and people assigned to the task could come and go within your organization. You may think you just need to create a digital brochure yourself in the next month, but it may morph into a two-part project including a printed version as well, requiring you to extend the deadline. Keep your plan streamlined, current, and handy so it can work hard for you.

AUDIOSOCKET

There's one final success story I want to share with you about the power of a marketing plan. Similar to GHGH, Audiosocket is an organization that grew organically at first. With more than 35,000 songs that span 204 genres of music, Audiosocket is a boutique music-licensing and technology company that gets music to people and companies who need it. The company represents more than 2,000 emerging bands, composers, and record labels from around the world.

Initially, the company relied solely on the success of its unique technology platform for delivering music to its customers. "In startup mode we had limited resources and were unable to get there any other way," says Jenn Miller, president & COO of Audiosocket. "But in this new stage of growth, we knew we needed more than a great product, we needed a strong marketing plan to take the business to the next level."

That realization really hit home when leading video sharing site Vimeo selected Audiosocket as a music partner for their Music Store. This was the first commercial implementation of Audiosocket's MaaS Platform. It gave Vimeo customers access to Audiosocket's complete song library to license and use as soundtracks for their video productions, with the ability to then distribute legally. On the flip side, Audiosocket's artists now had the benefit of a sizable new distribution channel including guaranteed royalty payments on all licensed music. They also gained exposure to Vimeo's more than 50 million monthly visitors—many of them professional filmmakers.[1]

With this major business deal, it was time for Audiosocket to amp up its marketing. "We knew we needed to drill down on a solid marketing and PR strategy to create awareness and drive sales, so one of the first structured activities we did was hire a reputable PR firm," says Jenn.

Audiosocket made the decision to outsource its media relations and hired a consulting firm to help create an action plan, and so far it has paid off. Its PR activities have directly led to a significant number of unique stories hitting the media and spin-off blogs. The company has also been featured in articles with headlines such as, "Top 10 Ways for Artists to Make Money." In addition to Vimeo, now Audiosocket is being approached by global media companies in digital, mobile, and content creation. Jenn says focusing time and resources on proactive PR and media planning helped put the company in the spotlight, and she knows investing more effort in marketing is the next step toward reaching the company's longer-term goals.

⟫   ⟫   ⟫

There's one final comment I want to make: In some cases you do need a more complex marketing plan. This could be when you're trying to secure a loan from a bank or other financial institution or if you plan to woo investors and make a formal pitch to a venture capital group. In these situations, you will likely need full details made available within a comprehensive business plan. Lenders and investors may need to see the details behind your marketing to be sure you have the right programs in place to reach your goals, make a reasonable profit, and pay any financial obligations.

⟫   ⟫   ⟫

Now you know what it takes to create the basics of a marketing action plan and make one work for you. As you've seen in this chapter, this powerful tool provides tremendous value to organizations of all sizes. The important thing to remember is that you're creating something simple to help you take action and produce results. Success in your planning efforts comes when you keep things streamlined and as easy as possible to manage. Taking time up front to create an action plan always pays off.

The Marketing Mindset

Take a few minutes to reflect on what you've read in this chapter and answer the following questions:

1. What type of marketing plan do you currently have in place?
2. What one marketing project would most benefit from an action plan?
3. What categories do you need to track?
4. What planning tool would work the best?
5. How will you ensure that the plan gets used regularly and adds value?

CHAPTER 9

Start Small and Grow Tall

In the last chapter, you clarified what you need to accomplish with your marketing by creating an action plan for your projects. But how do you get your ideas off the ground? How do you implement all of the good ideas in your plan and turn them into actions that get results? The easiest way to begin getting traction with your plan is to use what I call the "start small and grow tall" method. Some people might tell you to "go big or go home," but if you keep things simple from the get-go, chances are, you'll always stay on track and minimize your chances of failure. You need to create a simple process that works for you. Start with the most logical first small step, pounce on easy-to-do opportunities, and you'll start making things happen. Before you know it, the momentum will build and you'll be well on your way toward success with your marketing.

Having a simple sales and marketing process is key to success for both small and large organizations. On the large side of the spectrum, take Procter & Gamble (P&G), for example. With operations in about 80 countries, P&G's consumer goods are available in more than 180 countries worldwide. In 2011, P&G recorded $82.6 billion in sales, yet surprisingly, in order to achieve such massive results, the company uses a streamlined approach to its sales efforts.[1]

I had the good fortune to work with Ron Asahara, who spent more than 15 years in sales for P&G, and throughout the course of his career worked with many of the company's billon-dollar brands, including Olay, Crest, Vicks, Scope, and Pepto-Bismol. His role was to promote and sell those product lines to his customers: companies such as Wal-Mart, Target, Kmart, Kroger, Albertsons, and Walgreens. He shared with me behind-the-scenes stories demonstrating the brilliance behind P&G's basic sales process.

"One thing I have never forgotten from my P&G days is what we called 'The 5 Steps of Selling,'" says Ron. "Every P&G salesperson is taught to go through these when making a presentation to a buyer or customer, regardless of the size of the company." The 5 Steps are: Summarize the Situation, State the Idea, Explain How it Works, Reinforce Key Benefits, and Suggest Easy Next Steps. Ron says success lies in not just focusing on making the actual sales presentation, but doing the necessary preparation in advance.

"From my experience, I learned the importance of planning ahead and using a 'sales process' whether the outcome is favorable or not," says Ron. "There is always key information to learn along the way. I'd follow the process, document the information and feedback I'd get from the customers, and learn as much as I could from the sales call to better prepare and make any necessary changes before my next opportunity."

Ron is exactly right. As your marketing starts to move forward, it's important to pay close attention to what's working and what's not. That's the great thing about having a workable action plan: It's intended to be agile enough to let you adapt and make any necessary changes along the way. This makes the process much easier for you so you don't have to toss out the old plan and start over again if things change along the way. You just tweak your marketing activities and maximize all of your resources as you go along. Fortune 500 companies use this course-correcting method all the time, and it works especially well for small businesses, too. As I mentioned in the very beginning of the book, there's no one-size-fits-all marketing plan, but there is a proven process. If you carefully observe what is moving you forward and leverage the resources you have right at your fingertips, your marketing will get the right results for your organization.

COMPASSIONATE COOK

A great example of an entrepreneur who turned marketing ideas into action is Colleen Patrick-Goudreau. For more than 12 years, Colleen has guided people to becoming and staying vegan through sold-out cooking classes, best-selling books, inspiring lectures, engaging videos, and her popular audio podcast, "Vegetarian Food for Thought." Using her unique blend of passion, humor, and common sense, she empowers and inspires people to live according to their own values of compassion and wellness. Colleen attributes the success of her business to starting small and working her way up to this level through simple actions and maximizing every possible opportunity to help with her marketing. Because Colleen successfully built her business step by step, and was tremendously resourceful along the way, I think it's worth sharing her story in detail.

As a small business owner with extremely limited resources, Colleen had to keep things as simple as possible from the very beginning. "When I started my business I said to myself, 'This is what the need is and let me fill that need.' Even today, I don't do anything for its own sake. There has to be a reason and I have to see how it will help the public, as well as my business. And that's what has been the secret to my success."

At first, it was challenging to turn her ideas into actions that brought in a profit. "It's tricky for people like me who are running a business related to animal rights," she says. "It's vital work, but somehow there's the perception that if you're doing good work you can't take money for it because if you're making money you're a mercenary. It's a terrible model and it needs to change."

Throughout the years, Colleen found simple ways to maximize every resource within reach and grow her business. She said, "I'm really proud to have been able to create an effective business model that does good work in this world while providing me with a way to make a living doing it."

She used a straightforward approach to start gaining traction with her business. "The way I've done my work and grown my business from the very start is by identifying a problem, a public need in the market, and finding a way to provide the solution," she said. "It's as simple as that. I used the response of the people, listening to what they needed, to guide the direction of my business. And then I have literally taken advantage of every medium to provide that solution."

This is exactly how she started her business and began offering cooking classes. Passionate about the welfare of animals, she used to stand out on the street as an activist in Berkeley, California, handing out informational leaflets and showing videos of animals being mistreated by the farming industry.

"People would stop and say, 'I agree that this is horrible, but then what can I eat and how do I cook?' At that point, I said to myself, 'What they need is cooking lessons!' So I started teaching cooking classes. I wasn't a professionally trained chef—I have a masters degree in English Literature—but I just knew I had to start offering classes."

She found a great location, started offering her first courses, and launched her business. Colleen's experience expanded as she started teaching the classes, and she gathered a tremendous amount of knowledge about how best to use a vegan approach to traditional cooking techniques and make great-tasting meals. Her class participants valued the new information and gave her a perfect way to test her ideas and recipes. Interest in her tips and tools grew, and people started asking if she would make the classes and recipes available in other ways, especially for those living outside of the Bay Area.

"That's when I realized I needed to produce and promote a DVD. So I did," Colleen said. In this way, she successfully leveraged the content from her cooking classes and used it as building blocks to create a completely new line of business.

After the release of the DVD, Colleen continued to hear from people wanting even more access to her unique ideas and stories about how to cook in a more compassionate way. They asked if they could get more information online and through e-mail. Once again, she listened to the market, remained agile, and adjusted her course. Through her cooking classes, she knew she had a good method and voice for guiding people through the process of becoming vegan. But at this phase of her businesses growth, her time was very limited—as was her marketing budget. She decided to maximize her best resources and use them to help her share the information in the most simple and effective way possible. With just her computer and a microphone, she created a series of podcasts and started promoting them on her Website.

"I sat down and recorded the first podcast six years ago," she said. "I didn't know much about creating an effective podcast, how to market it, or if anyone would listen when I was starting it. I knew my content was really strong. I just did it and put it out there and my customer base found me. When I saw it was working, that people were responding well to me using that format, I just kept doing it and the word of mouth started to grow and spread. The podcast enabled me to tap into an audience I had never had before: an international audience. That was very powerful."

People found Colleen's information so significant and life-changing that another business model grew around it, enabling her to build incremental revenue she could use to better promote the podcast. What started as a grassroots way to say thank you grew into a full-fledged sponsorship program.

"I literally started getting checks in the mail in the first couple of months of doing the podcast," she said. "Something was working. People would write to me and say, 'You have to keep this going, this is so amazing! What can I do to support you?' That's how the revenue model for the podcast began. I started what I called the Podcast Sponsorship Program."

In the podcast itself, Colleen started reading these letters from people who were saying they were finding real value from her podcast. She'd then invite her other listeners to do the same and become a podcast sponsor. "People value what they pay for, and, like the public radio or public television model, people who see value in the podcast literally make it possible."

Eventually she decided not to limit sponsorships to her podcasts. She tweaked the original idea and created a comprehensive membership program with three participation levels and cost structures. "There's tons of content that's free on my Website," she said. "And the podcast is still free, but if people want premium content (recipes, videos, essays) from me, they see the value, know it is helping make the world a better place, and are willing to pay for extra support and information."

Colleen continues to stay nimble with her business and her marketing. She evolved the sponsorship program through the years to include businesses and organizations into what is now called the Compassionate Business Partners Program. Funding comes from local and national organizations that support her brand and compassionate cause. Today her partners include Vegan Essentials, Earth Balance, Arbonne, Dr. Fuhrman, Boston Baked Bonz, and Cinnaholic, a vegan gourmet cinnamon roll company.

Turning her ideas into action hasn't always been easy. Colleen has hit a few speed bumps and taken a few detours. "I've had a few offshoots. There have been times along the way when I went in one direction and my gut and all signs pointed to 'No, that's not the way to go.' I had to listen to that gut, not force it, and go back to the core of what's the most effective and what's also supporting me in revenue. I have to continue to ask myself, 'What's the best use of my time?' because I have limited resources."

One of the offshoots Colleen explored was creating a training program to certify Compassionate Cook instructors around the world. It made perfect sense at the time to evolve her 10 years of teaching classes into a school as well respected as the Culinary Institute of America. After speaking with an attorney about how to structure the school and whether or not it would be better to create a franchise model, she suddenly recognized it would be better to keep things simple.

"I realized my greatest skills and strengths are in cooking, teaching, writing, and speaking, and it was a complete waste of my time and effort to head in this new direction," she said.

Today, by sticking to her vision and streamlining her efforts, Colleen has built an impressive business. An award-winning author, she's written three cookbooks—*The Joy of Vegan Baking, The Vegan Table*, and *Color Me Vegan*—and two vegan/compassionate living books—*Vegan's Daily Companion* and *The 30-Day Vegan Challenge*. She has also appeared on the Food Network and PBS, and is a regular contributor to National Public Radio and *The Christian Science Monitor*. Through her sold-out cooking classes, inspiring lectures, and immensely popular audio podcast, "Vegetarian Food for Thought," she continues to guide people to live as healthfully and compassionately as possible.

My goal in sharing Colleen's business journey with you is to demonstrate the process of turning ideas into action. Her story is a perfect example of how one simple step can lead to the next, and of the power that comes from maximizing every resource available. As I mentioned earlier, you'll get great results if you start small by keeping things as simple and manageable as possible. All of those little activities will add up and take your business to the next level.

10 WAYS TO LEVERAGE YOUR ASSETS

As you begin to use your plan, it's important to identify your most easily accessible resources. What's right at your fingertips and within reach? These opportunities are often the best-kept secrets that can and do make a big difference in accomplishing more with your marketing. Following are 10 simple ways to leverage your assets and put them to work for you.

1. Maximize Your Time

You can get a lot of marketing done in a short amount of time. When you start using your action plan, just 15 minutes of work can pay off in a very big way. This happened for Brett Renville, that cinematographer and fashion photographer I mentioned back in Chapter 1. Here's the story behind how he was hired by the NGO Kageno: He sent an e-mail. It was that straightforward.

"After having the chance to film and make a difference in Haiti, I'd been wanting to do more humanitarian work," said Brett. In between editing films for his clients, Brett took a break and flipped through a copy of *Vogue* magazine. "I came across a story about a supermodel working with an NGO in Africa called Kegano that was helping to transform impoverished African villages." After doing some quick research on the organization's Website, he sent an e-mail. "I didn't overthink it. I sent a very short note saying I wanted to work with them, and if they needed any film or photography work done, to let me know. The president e-mailed me right back the next day."

Within a week, Brett was booked on a flight to Rwanda.

2. Repackage Your Knowledge

If you have built up a wealth of information about your product or service, use it to your advantage in as many ways possible. This works extremely well for service-based businesses, as you saw in Colleen's story. She was able to take information from her cooking classes and turn it into an effective DVD. From there, she rolled what she knew into podcasts and eventually used her proven recipes and advice to create award-winning cookbooks. Use the information you already have at your fingertips by packaging it in new ways to create more value for your customers and deliver more revenue for you.

A big mistake I see so many people make is reinventing the wheel when it comes to their marketing. There are many times when you can and should reuse what you already have, especially when it comes to your communication methods such as Websites and e-mail.

I recently worked with a financial services company led by a terrific writer. She spent hours writing a how-to blog post and it turned out to be a terrific article. I asked why she wasn't pitching that story to a magazine or converting it to a press release to send to other media outlets. So she did those things and it was picked up as a story in a national business magazine.

Some situations require you to create something new—for example, when the material is outdated or your brand or company has evolved. But in many cases, the best material is right at your fingertips, so try to make the most of what you already have at your disposal.

3. Jump on Lasting Trends

Most trends come and go, but some stay the course and manage to shift our thinking. Throughout the years, "sustainability" has grown from a trendy topic to a mindset that's here to stay. One business that embraced this early was the Pan Pacific Hotels Group, a boutique chain of luxury hotels around the world. Beyond just implementing a few green initiatives, Pan Pacific's Seattle hotel created a comprehensive global responsibility initiative called the "PanEarth Program." Creating this program positioned the Seattle property as a thought leader within its industry. From housekeeping to management, all staff members—or "associates," as the hotel calls its team members—are involved in making a positive impact on the environment while caring for guests during their stay.

"We offer a complete PanEarth Ambassador certification program to any interested associate who wants to learn more," says David Sullivan, general manager of the hotel. "Once they have demonstrated their knowledge, they are empowered to take anyone from guests to members of the media on a full, back-of-the-house tour to see the program in action, from low-flush toilets to the more than 100 pounds of soap we donate each month to Clean the World." Sullivan has more than 25 years in the hospitality business and has worked for major brands including Four Seasons Hotels and Resorts and the Regent Hotel in London, U.K. "We've made a long-term commitment to be sustainably responsible and will continue to invest in the PanEarth program because it's not only critical for the environment, but it also benefits our guests and associates, and it is the right thing to do from a business perspective."

4. Create an Internship Program

One tremendously helpful resource many people forget about is interns. Creating an internship program, whether for college credit or not, is one of the best things you can do to move your marketing forward. As a university professor, I can't tell you how many students I have each year who are desperate to add some real-world marketing experience to their resume. And career centers at universities and colleges are always looking for new internships they can make available to their students.

An intern can work as little as five hours a week or as much as full-time, depending on your needs and the student's availability. Paid internships usually start at minimum wage—that said, you don't have to pay an intern, but you do need to create a compelling work opportunity. It has to be something that will help the intern learn. I recently helped a creative agency create an internship program and one-page job description. Within a week, the founder had a student ready and willing to help with everything from managing social media to pitching news stories to the media. Creating an internship position is a great way to help your organization *and* help a student.

5. Leverage the People Around You, Especially Employees

In May 2000, the U.S. government made a decision to make a broader range of GPS signals available to civilians. Within 24 hours, Dave Ulmer placed the first geocache (at that time called a "GPS Stash") in Oregon and posted its coordinates online. Three days later, Mike Teague used a personal GPS receiver to find it. After discovering the "Original Stash," he shared his experiences with the burgeoning community online.

Four months later, a guy named Jeremy Irish launched Geocaching. com to support the hobby. A few weeks after that, *The New York Times* covered it on the front of the Circuits section and the site was inundated with visitors. To get some help supporting the site, Jeremy asked his "real job" coworkers, Elias Alvord and Bryan Roth, to join him, and the three men founded Groundspeak. To this day, the company continues to involve employees in the growth of the business and support its mission to inspire outdoor play using location-based technology. It even has a catalog of videos of employee and customer real-world stories on its Website, demonstrating everyone's clear passion for the game.

This authentic form of relationship-based marketing is key to Groundspeak's success. "After one year at Groundspeak, all employees get to go travel to meet the geocaching community at geocaching events," says cofounder Bryan.

Where exactly they go depends on their seniority, based on years at the company, but everyone gets a chance to travel somewhere in the world. "By sending our team members on customer-facing trips, the employee has some fun with our customers, gets a motivation boost, and brings that positive experience and frontline knowledge back to the company," says Bryan. "It helps us constantly stay on top of what our community wants and allows us to help share their geocaching stories and experiences."

6. Get More out of Your Social Media

The art industry continues to evolve, and with the rise of social media, more and more artists are taking their sales and marketing into their own hands to build relationships with their base of fans and collectors. Josh Keyes is one of those artists—and he just so happens to be my brother. Infused with stunning images of lifelike animals and slices of landscape, Josh's style of painting is reminiscent of scientific textbook illustrations with a twist of concerned playfulness about the Earth's future.

As most artists do, Josh started his career struggling to show and sell his work. In an effort to grow his business, he teamed up with galleries and nonprofit organizations to give his paintings more visibility. In the past

20 years, he's worked hard to build an impressive, active, and vocal group. They include more than 5,000 Facebook followers, active participants in online art chat rooms and forums, and even more fans in his e-mail database. Today his paintings sell almost instantly, even before the paint has time to dry—no small feat for a small business owner. Every minute he steps away from his studio is time he could be creating another painting.

For this reason, social media has become an essential part of the marketing process for Josh. "Social media tools save me a lot of time and give my supporters an easy way to stay connected to me and my process," he said. Looking for ways to meet the growing needs of his supporters, Josh began releasing limited-edition fine art prints. With each release comes a surge of people blogging and sharing information about the upcoming print through social media channels. "For my most recent release, instead of selecting the image to be used for the print myself, I decided to start an online poll both on Facebook and other art forums, and let my fans vote for their favorite image," says Josh.

It was an incredible success for both Josh and his base of collectors. "As an artist, I may have an original idea about what's interesting, but so much depends on the people who are ultimately going to buy it and hang it on their wall." Thanks to the power of social media buzz, combined with Josh's own mailing list efforts, more than 300 of the prints sold out in five minutes. In this way, he is using social media in innovative ways to move his business forward, and is becoming a pioneer in the art industry.

7. Use Your Personal Strengths

Of course you can't always do the things you want to do, especially when you're in startup mode in your business or facing crunch time on a big project. Even if you don't like it or aren't good at it, you may have to do everything from producing a video to creating a social media campaign for a while. But as soon as possible, start incorporating your passions and strengths into your marketing. This directly ties back to the situational analysis you completed in Chapter 2. If you can tap into what you're good at, your marketing will be much more effective.

Whenever I think about tapping into personal strengths, I reflect back on a contact of mine who used to work at a large corporation. She was a terrific marketer and quickly worked her way up the corporate ladder, eventually ending up as a director for a team that handled the company's most prized possessions: its biggest customers around the world. She did everything expected of her and more: produced articles about the customers, managed events, wrote press releases, created slide decks—you name it, she did it. She was smart and strategic, and excelled at marketing research and analysis. She always knew what it would take to help the company shine in front of its best customers.

One day, her manager, the vice president, walked into her office and gave her a huge promotional opportunity. "I've got something I want you to do that will give you tremendous visibility and career growth," he said. He wanted her to speak in front of a group of 500 of the company's inside sales and marketing people. There was only one catch: She was an introvert. The thought of speaking in front of a group of 10 her coworkers, let alone 500 strangers, was terrifying. She thanked him for the big break, but explained her situation and said she would gladly work behind the scenes to help create a dynamic presentation he or someone else on the team could deliver.

But he wouldn't take no for an answer. He wanted her to do it. "It will help your career," he prodded. "You need to build those skills; you need to improve your strengths in public speaking if you want to get ahead." She promptly quit the company.

If only her manager had paid attention to her strengths, valued what she was good at, and supported her in what she did best, she might still be with his company. Instead, she now runs a successful strategic marketing consulting company with a Fortune-500 client, making far more money and using all of her greatest assets to do exactly the things she is best at doing. This is one of the easiest and most pleasurable ways to move your business forward.

8. Integrate as Much as Possible

With more than 40 percent of coffee drinkers in the United States preferring a lighter coffee taste, Starbucks needed to find a way to better serve existing and potential new customers by offering a milder, less intense coffee option. Eighteen months and 80 different roast and recipe iterations later, they landed on the perfect roast profile: Starbucks Blonde Roast. To reach customers across all of the company's distribution channels—its retail stores, companies licensing the Starbucks brand, and other locations where people buy groceries—with a cohesive message, Starbucks brought all of its marketing and PR resources together in a fast, effective way to deliver the right business results. It was the first time in its history that the company simultaneously launched a new product in its retail stores and grocery channels globally.

Because the new product required Starbucks, known for its signature dark roast, to educate customers about its new Blonde Roast, the marketing team introduced a series of taste tests, called "Find the Roast You Love Most." According to Alisa Martinez, senior communications manager for Starbucks, the company used its retail footprint to reach hundreds of thousands of customers in several days so they could sample a coffee from each of Starbucks' roast categories—Blonde, Medium, and Dark—to determine their favorite. With this taste challenge, the company wanted its customers to affirm their taste preferences or discover new ones. Starbucks then provided customers with a $1 off coupon toward one pound of whole bean coffee. They were also given a free tasting guide showcasing the coffee roast categories and a sticker identifying them by their preferred roast.

As part of the campaign, Starbucks implemented a comprehensive, multi-phased PR strategy, which included long-lead outreach with consumer publications, a five-city business announcement featuring Starbucks executives and coffee experts, and a launch day announcement. Finally, "Find the Roast You Love Most" media and blogger events were held at signature Starbucks stores in three cities soon after launch. In the end, Starbucks achieved 287 million media impressions from the business announcement, 250 million media impressions from the consumer announcement, and 95 percent message pull-through. The company continues to leverage its retail stores and store partners (employees), as well as its 30 million Facebook fans and millions of registered Starbucks Card holders around the world to help tell its story and drive awareness of Starbucks Blonde Roast and its Roast Spectrum.

So far, Blonde Roast is exceeding Starbucks' original forecasts down grocery store aisles as well as in its retail stores. By completely integrating its marketing, the company not only generated awareness for the new product, but also proved its customers could now get a high-quality, great-tasting cup of light roast coffee.

9. Work Your Testimonials

I'm always surprised at the number of businesspeople who tell me they have a folder of positive feedback from customers. Testimonials are great, but they don't do you much good if you keep them filed away in a folder in your inbox, and thank-you cards full of kudos don't help your marketing if they're stashed somewhere in your desk. Take those positive words and use them somewhere—anywhere. You can share that feedback on your Website, include it in your e-newsletter, tweet about it, or post a few of those words of praise on Facebook. You don't have to worry about getting permission unless you plan to use the person's full name.

10. Recycle Your Tools

From fliers to slide presentations, effective marketing often involves a variety of communication tools. There's no reason you can't repurpose ones that work well or revamp the ones that aren't working. Lisa Stratton is a senior marketing manager for Microsoft, responsible for the strategy and execution behind customer relationship marketing programs for the Windows Phone. She found a great way to reuse an ineffective e-mail campaign tool. In her role, Lisa helps customers learn to use the phone, discover new features, and ultimately decide they can't live without it. No small task. According to Lisa, it's an exciting time to be in the Windows Phone business because of Microsoft's recent partnership with Nokia. "There's a great opportunity to really expand this category in new ways with Nokia and our other smartphone partners," she said.

That said, Lisa acknowledges that Microsoft is "a little late to the smartphone party," with iPhone and Android having already having established themselves in the marketplace. "We're working hard to win the hearts and minds of customers as they learn more about why Windows Phone is better, like Live tiles that bring their phone's Start screen to life, and app integration to help people do things much faster on the device," she said.

A major focus for Lisa is creating effective e-mail campaigns that add value for her customers. As with any ongoing marketing, Lisa needs to create a high-quality, interesting publication month after month, on budget, with a limited amount of resources. "Often, there is late-breaking information we need to include in our e-mail, and it requires us to be nimble and turn things around very quickly," she said.

Using a template for promotional e-mail is a great way to streamline the process, but Lisa says the trouble with templates is they tend to look stale after a while, and there are usually design limitations requiring you to choose the "best options available," which are not always the "best one for the job."

"The existing e-mail template I inherited when I joined the team was so limited; every single e-mail looked the same, with the headline and main image and story article—what I call a 'hero'—in the same place, and then three sub-articles below it," Lisa said. "Since we'd always have a photo of a phone in our hero article, probably the only person who noticed the difference between the e-mails was me!"

To get better results from her e-mail tool and keep the marketing process simple, Lisa worked with her agency to refresh the template and make it much more flexible. "What we came up with is the best e-mail template I've used in my 14 years at Microsoft because it's easy for the creative agency to work with and doesn't limit their creativity," she said. "We have five different modules that we can choose to include—or not—in each e-mail we send," she said. In one module, Lisa can change the entire layout, and in the others, she uses visuals—product images, screenshots, and mobile app tiles—within the set templates to change the look each month. In this way, she ensures every e-mail looks different, yet is consistent. "The e-mail coder loves it because she can reuse code in each issue, instead of having to rebuild a new e-mail from scratch every time," Lisa said. "That is really important because it's always her time that gets condensed when information comes in late and we can't move the send date." It's also consistent enough so Lisa's customers know they can trust the content, and look forward to items in each new issue. "And most important, it is driving great results for opens, clicks and shares."

With the previous template, Lisa and her team needed four to six weeks to create each new e-mail, from the first briefing with her agency to the time the piece was sent to customers. This time frame included the agency writing the content and designing the creative treatment, then Lisa having to route the proposed e-mail through three rounds of reviews with key stakeholders and management, a legal review, and finally the HTML building and testing of the e-mail. "Using the new template," she said, "we can do it in as little as four days, if needed, but our start-to-finish time for this marketing campaign has been cut in half just by redesigning that original e-mail template."

⏭   ⏭   ⏭

As I hope I've shown you in this chapter, the best way to start turning your marketing plan into real action is to take things one piece at a time and develop a process that works for you. As you begin implementing the ideas in your plan, be as resourceful as possible every step of the way. Try to identify from among the resources you have at hand those that are most easily accessible. By doing this, you'll maximize your time and stretch your budget and other resources. I've never seen a plan implemented perfectly from the first step to the last, because things always change. By the time you're midway through your plan, there will likely be a new social media tool, or something will happen in the news and there's a new trend worth investigating. That's why it's good to take things bit by bit. Remember: Start small and grow tall.

The Marketing Mindset

Take a few minutes to reflect on what you've read in this chapter and answer the following questions.

1. What's your current process for turning your marketing plan and ideas into action?

2. What are three underutilized resources you have at your fingertips?

3. How can you maximize your time? Is there something you can do in just 15 minutes that might move your business forward?

4. Are there ways you can better leverage the people around you, especially your employees?

5. How can you get more out of your marketing tools and activities? Are there ways you can repackage your knowledge and information? Do you have any marketing content you can reuse? Can you do more with your social media?

PART V

SPEED:
Accelerate and Move Forward

Large is no longer in charge.... Leverage will belong to the nimble and the swift.

—Sumner Redstone

Throughout this book, I've shared with you the principles of Strategy, Story, Strength, and Simplicity, and how they all work together to fuel your marketing and move your business forward. In this last part of the book, I'll show you how the final principle, Speed, can lead you to great success in two ways: first, by taking advantage of opportunities as they arise, and second, by swiftly gathering the right results through measurement and analysis.

Chapter 10 covers numerous topics to help you put the pedal to the metal without jeopardizing the quality of your efforts. You'll learn the value of tracking your progress and how to quickly assess what isn't working for your marketing. From the information you gain, you'll be able to see what *is* effective so you can fine-tune even more to get the most out of your efforts. Finally, I'll show you how to look beyond merely a financial return on your investment to how your results can also make a broader, positive impact.

Any business or organization that's finely tuned and agile is able to make on-the-fly adjustments to stay on course and get results quickly. After reading this final section on Speed, you'll be on your way to success in no time.

CHAPTER 10

Get Results—Fast

I ALWAYS HAVE MIXED feelings when a marketing campaign comes to an end. Whether it's a Website redesign, a social media audit, or a global product launch, I thrive on the feeling of accomplishment and getting a sense of closure. At the same time, I can't wait to roll up my sleeves and start figuring out if it was effective or not. You may be glad to have all of the planning and implementation behind you, but there's still some work to be done and excitement to be had as you chase down the end results. You need to be sure your effort paid off and your marketing led to outcomes that will truly benefit your business. Once you have that behind you, it's time to acknowledge the lessons you learned and celebrate your successes.

Many organizations skip this important phase of their marketing programs and miss a tremendous opportunity to reflect on what went well and what could be improved. They put a lot of effort and resources into their marketing up front but then never evaluate it. They jump for joy after being featured on a top blog but neglect to find out if any new business came from the online mention. Hopefully it went well, but you won't really know until you do some analysis and take a hard look at the results.

Getting accurate data quickly is key. You don't want to lose your momentum or forget the details. That's why it's important to capture things while they are fresh in your mind. It's crucial to take a look at your results along the way to see if they are in line with what you hoped to accomplish. Only then will you know if your marketing took you to the next level.

ALASKA AIRLINES—TAX RELIEF

A fascinating example of a corporation that did a great job of monitoring its marketing progress is Alaska Airlines. On Friday, July 22, 2011, Congress missed an important deadline that prevented the government from extending a bill to keep the Federal Aviation Administration (FAA) running. This temporary loss of the FAA's ability to impose various federal taxes to airlines created a window in which customers could purchase tickets without having to pay those taxes. As a result, the federal government started losing an estimated $25 million a day in tax revenue.[1]

Many airlines immediately raised their fares (in some cases within 24 hours) to fill the gap, keeping what would have been the tax money and pocketing anywhere from $25 to $50 per round trip ticket. But Alaska Airlines saw this as a chance to act quickly and pass the benefit directly to its customers by offering lower fares. It acted swiftly to create an impressive strategic marketing campaign to differentiate itself from the airlines that took the windfall. By doing what was best for its customers, the company positioned itself as an industry leader.

Within 24 hours from first getting word of the issue, Alaska started its marketing engines to explore this unique opportunity. Vice president of marketing Joe Sprague sprang into action and asked his team to find a way to pass the savings to customers during this "tax holiday" of sorts. One of Joe's team members, Kelli Goss, was involved in helping to produce and launch what resulted in a clever "temporary tax relief" marketing campaign in record time.

"From the speed to market on the original decision, to creative concepts and approvals, to actually advertising this was *extremely* fast!" says Kelli Goss, e-commerce manager for Alaska Airlines. "When the decision was made, we kicked into high gear."

Following is a simplified timeline captured by Kelli of the first few hours and days as the company rapidly implemented its marketing plans.

July 21, 2011

@ Midday—all U.S. airlines notified Congress would likely not pass an extension and taxes would expire on July 23 at midnight

July 22, 2011

@ 12:28 p.m.—VP of marketing e-mailed me to find out how fast we could turn around an online ad on the company's Website if we decided to publicize our savings to customers

@ 12:34 p.m.—I sent an e-mail to my Web designer and to our campaign management manager to get this campaign in motion

@ 12:36 p.m.—the campaign manager sent us a tracking code for the ad and started on the process of creating a campaign request, which allows us to add in all details on a campaign. We have a call daily where all advertising teams call in to review how we can work together to market the campaign

@ 1:04 p.m.—our media relations manager e-mailed us to ask about details for a press release

@ 3:17 p.m.—our senior graphic designer had four concepts for me to review

@ 3:26 p.m.—our media relations manager e-mailed us a draft message to send to the media and asked us to review it

@ 3:34 p.m.—VP and I made the decision to go with the "boy and the abacus" concept for our ads. It was quirky and eye-catching. The boy reminded us of a kid pretending to be a tax accountant and the abacus of a counting tool on how much customers would save

@ 4:08 p.m.—our tax manager signed off on the verbiage and proposed landing page copy to explain to customers what they would be saving specifically

@ 5:30 p.m.—we had a landing page coded and ready to deploy at midnight along with the banner ad for our home page on alaskaair.com

<u>July 23</u>

@ Midnight—we published the ad and landing pages and all of the savings were passed on to the customers

Alaska Airlines passed on savings to its customers for 16 days until the FAA taxes were reinstated. Acting swiftly in that short amount of time was extremely effective in generating revenue for the airline from additional sales, but perhaps a more important result was the ability to convey the company's "customers first" brand values. More than 60 broadcast stories ran the first day the tax holiday was announced, reaching nearly 3 million people, followed by dozens of other media hits in print and online outlets nationwide and overseas. All of them positioned Alaska Airlines as an industry leader, doing the right thing for its customers. This is an impressive example of corporate responsibility, as well as exceptional marketing agility.

➠ ➠ ➠

It's clear from this Alaska Airlines story that being able to act quickly and respond immediately to changing dynamics is crucial. The sooner you can get in front of an opportunity, the better chance you have at succeeding with your marketing. And once your activities come to a close, this need for speed becomes even more important. You've got to capture the lessons learned in a timely manner and evaluate whether or not what you did worked and if you got the results you needed.

NOT GETTING RESULTS?

Speaking of results, one of the biggest complaints I hear people make is, "Why isn't my marketing working?" They usually have put a great deal of effort into a specific activity and aren't getting the results they desperately need. A few examples I've heard throughout the years include:

- Sending an idea for a how-to article to several magazines and not hearing back from a single editor
- Producing an interesting video, posting it to YouTube, and only getting 100 views
- Coming up with a clever tweet that isn't retweeted

It's easy to think if you're not getting results that your marketing isn't working, but the marketing itself may not be the problem. There are other three reasons why you might not be getting results:

1. It Could Be You

Yes, it can happen: You may have taken a misstep with your marketing. That's okay; you're human. Now is a perfect time to be objective as you reflect on the process you used and the quality of your work. Using the example of a how-to article, maybe you created content in your media pitch that was full of typos or came across as more of an ad for your business instead of an article that would help inform a magazine's readers. Could you have made it a bit more polished, more compelling, and more focused on a unique news story angle? If this is the case—if the problem comes down to you—then take a clear look at your work, compare it to other activities you've performed that have gotten results, and do what it takes to make it better. If your output isn't up to snuff, then you need to boost its quality.

2. It Might Be Them

Maybe your work *is* good enough and you can point the finger at someone else. It could be that the magazine editor was extremely busy hiring a new employee the day you sent your e-mail. Or her child was sent home sick from school. It could be that the editor didn't like your idea for whatever reason and deleted it as soon as she read the subject line of your e-mail. Or perhaps she was multitasking and accidentally deleted your e-mail. You can try to guess the reason, but you may never know. In this case, you have to let it go.

3. It Could Be Something Completely Unexpected

When I worked at Microsoft, I was pitching a news story to *The Oprah Winfrey Show* about how a woman was using MSN Messenger to stay connected with her husband during the Iraq war. It was a moving story of how technology was bridging the physical divide between this husband and wife. The producer loved the story and we were all set to go and feature the wife on the show when one of the producers e-mailed back with a last-minute change. An injured soldier who had lost his leg in the line of duty had just been flown home and the producer had the opportunity to share his story on the show. His story needed to be told and was far more compelling to Oprah's viewers than our technology-based idea. It wasn't us, and it wasn't them; it was something completely unexpected and out of our control.

⟫   ⟫   ⟫

Whatever the reason your marketing isn't working, you need to get to the bottom of it. This is why it's so valuable to take time to monitor your progress throughout a campaign and especially assess the end game. Some people think there's no point in evaluating marketing, especially social media. I recently heard a marketing expert interviewed on the radio, and he was comparing marketing to his grandmother's cookies. He said something along the lines of, "Her cookies are just plain good, and there's no way to measure that. The same is true for Twitter."

I can't argue with the power of that gut feeling, and it's an especially good guide in determining the deliciousness of a cookie. But you do need to go with more than just your gut to measure the effectiveness of your marketing. If the family stops eating grandma's cookies for some reason, what's the point in her continuing to spend her extra money to buy ingredients and take time to bake them? Chances are, she would want to get to the bottom of why those cookies got left on the platter.

RETURN ON INVESTMENT AND IMPACT

You need to get to the bottom of this question as quickly as possible. After all of your effort, and the time and money you invested, was your marketing worth it? What level of response did you get? Should you or should you not repeat the same efforts? What was the ultimate value of what you did? Was it beneficial? These questions are all related to the return on your investment (ROI).

ROI refers to how much revenue you received compared with the investment you put into the given project. For years this was how we measured success in the corporate world: all from the bottom line. It used to be an assessment of what revenue you spent and your overall investment of time and money. If a project required two employees and their time for two days and you paid them $10 per hour, and you had them working eight hours, that's $160 times 2, or $320. If you made $400 on the project, you made money, and if you only made $300, you lost money. So dollar for dollar, hour for hour, how did you do? If you invested $25,000 in marketing your product, did you earn that back—or more? Are you in the black when it comes to your bottom line?

It's a simple concept, but success can't always be measured in such a clear, black-and-white way. It isn't always so cut and dried. Today, many organizations measure success not only by revenue, but also by the positive impact of their efforts, as was true in the Alaska Airlines case. How did your marketing program make a positive difference for your company, your customers, and, in some cases, even the world at large? This is a much more intangible result that's tricky to quantify, but important nonetheless to be aware of and to evaluate. "Return on investment" has evolved into "return on investment plus impact," and the results you're able to achieve for your organization, through marketing, can affect much more than just the bottom line.

INVISIBLE CHILDREN, INC.

Invisible Children, Inc., is a nonprofit group that used social media to rally people worldwide against Ugandan guerilla group leader Joseph Kony. The group posted a 30-minute video to YouTube regarding Kony's recruiting of children as soldiers in his army,[2] and the video went viral immediately. As I'll show you, the group had a simple plan that worked incredibly well and delivered immediate results, both from a return on investment and positive impact.

I first learned of the group when two of my Seattle University students told me about the video in class. "Millions of people around the world have watched it in the past two days," they exclaimed. "You've got to watch it as soon as possible. Do it tonight!" And so I did.

The film was produced as part of an educational marketing campaign by Invisible Children, and within the first few minutes of the video, Invisible Children's vision was crystal clear: Use the power of social media and pop culture to turn Kony into a "celebrity" of sorts, and in that way, bring mass awareness to this horrific issue, leading to necessary political action and ultimately the arrest of Kony. The story is directed and narrated by Invisible Children cofounder Jason Russell, and juxtaposes shots of his young son in California with images of the hopelessness of African children. Jason explains how Joseph Kony has abducted roughly 60,000 children in the past 10 years, and how Invisible Children intends to use the film, along with social action, to end the use of child soldiers and the destruction of families and communities in Uganda.

The campaign was working. Teen idol Justin Bieber retweeted an Invisible Children message and looped the link to the video to his 18-million-plus followers, saying, "It is time to make him known. I'm calling on ALL MY FANS, FRIENDS, and FAMILY to come together and #STOPKONY. This is not a joke. This is serious. TOGETHER we can #MakeAChange and #STOPKONY—help another kid in need!"[3]

Oprah, who has more than 9 million followers on Twitter alone, referenced Kony's Lord's Resistance Army, saying, "Thanks tweeps for sending me info about ending #LRAviolence. I am aware. Have supported with $'s and voice and will not stop. #KONY2012."[4]

In addition to the video, Invisible Children also created an action kit for sale on the organization's Website for $30.[5] The box was promoted with a marketing message saying, "People will think you're an advocate of awesome. Everything you'll need to take part in our KONY 2012 campaign is included in this kit: an official campaign." The kit included a T-shirt, a KONY bracelet, an action guide, stickers, a button, and posters.

On the surface, the viral marketing of the video worked brilliantly. The film got more than 55 million views on YouTube in the first three days and received worldwide media recognition. Even the kit sold out immediately and went straight into backorder status from the immense popularity of the movement.

But throughout the course of the next few days, skeptics started critiquing Invisible Children's motives.[6] Along with the immense popularity of the video and impressive effort by the filmmakers to raise awareness of an African tragedy came an inundation of questions about the organization's intentions, its financial transparency, and whether the social media fury was too little, too late for the Ugandan people. Kony and his army had left the region, and according to some reports, were now only leading a small band of 100 people. In addition, the organization received unwanted media coverage and additional public criticism when Jason, the cofounder featured in the film, was hospitalized on March 15. His health was reportedly jeopardized from exhaustion, dehydration, and malnutrition.[7] The campaign continued to move forward despite these challenges, and on April 20, 2012, another phase of marketing activities began. On that date, people around the world turned their passion into action and enacted a "Cover the Night" campaign with posters of Kony's face. Unfortunately, the movement's initial viral success with the video didn't translate into as much real-world action across the globe as the organization had hoped.[8]

Whether you agree or disagree with the course this marketing campaign has run, there are a lot of lessons to be learned. What makes this case study a marketing wonder is the lightning speed of the results as they unfolded, especially the YouTube views and tweets. The fact that so many people are electronically "connected" these days allows social media to be a fast-acting circuit for change. But time will tell what the long-term impact of this marketing campaign will be on the organization's brand and if in fact Invisible Children is able to reach its organizational goal of bringing Joseph Kony to justice.

MONITORING AND ANALYZING YOUR RESULTS

It's extremely important to pay close attention to what's happening at every step of your marketing program and capture the results along the way. As an effective marketer, you must go back and remember how you got from start to finish during your project, so it's wise to establish a good process from the start, and use it consistently throughout the program. That said, you don't want to over-track, by either making the process a burden or by gathering information that is of no use. Try to find a balance where you make note of only the most valuable details about your marketing efforts—those that will benefit your analysis later.

You should do your analysis as soon as you have the results in hand, while everything is fresh in your mind. Have you ever been part of a brainstorming session in which you write a bunch of thoughts on a flip chart? Then months later, when you need to look back at the notes for some reason, you scratch your head and wonder, "What the heck did this mean?" They were important observations at the time, but it can be hard to reassemble those details, especially when huge sheets of paper and multicolored pens are involved.

Most large corporations track every bit of customer data they can get their hands on and many are going so far as to attach all internal spending to the value it generates in customer sales. For example, after making a purchase at Target, you'll find a user ID and password near the bottom of your receipt. You're encouraged to visit targetsurvey.com to spend a few minutes giving the company feedback about your recent shopping experience. In exchange for your time, you get a 10-percent-off coupon to use the next time you shop at the store. Although smart and admirable, this can involve millions of dollars in software development and database management. As I've mentioned throughout the book, your marketing efforts don't have to be that complicated. If you don't have access to that level of budget and resources, there are other methods you can use to quickly and efficiently measure your marketing.

One way is to start with a strategic review meeting. At Microsoft, following any major marketing project, we held what we called a "postmortem." It's a medical term used to describe the examination done on someone who has passed away to determine the cause of death. In our case, it referred to the post-campaign discussion we'd have in which we would dissect every aspect of what went well and what didn't. Within a week after the program came to a close, we would gather everyone involved and go through the details. This was somewhat of a 360-degree debriefing, and often included sales leads in other countries, external vendors, and in some cases even customers and partners. Around the table and through the conference call system we would go, asking everyone to share observations about what went well and what didn't go well. All feedback was welcome, whether it was positive, negative, or neutral. In these meetings, we would go back to the very start, revisiting our corporate vision as well as our specific business goals and marketing objectives. I would always have my marketing plan in front of me and go through it line by line so no stone was left unturned.

In some ways, you could say this quick review is similar to the SWOT analysis you did at the start of this book in Chapter 2; only this time, it's more of an excavation you're doing for a specific marketing campaign. At Microsoft, someone was assigned to take notes on a laptop and collect them in a spreadsheet with all the critical details, saving them so we could repeat the good things and do our best to turn the negatives into positives the next time around. The important thing was, we got everything out on the table and looked at it together with open minds and constructively critical eyes. We weren't afraid to identify what didn't work. With hindsight, we learned plenty of lessons and evolved our failures into gems.

As I've demonstrated throughout this book, one of the quickest data-collection and analysis tools you can create is a simple grid in Excel or Word. Here's an example of a high-level one I might have completed back when I worked at Microsoft:

Activities	Positive Outcomes	Lessons Learned
Strategy: Vision to objectives, situation	Clear vision and goals	Didn't have enough data on competitive landscape
Story: Brand, messaging, and target audience	Brand attributes were consistent in all marketing	Uncovered new niche market, but marketing messages didn't resonate
Strength: Customers, partner, and media	Good support from 93% of partners	Some confusion in media with competition's messaging
Simplicity: Action plan	Online registration process worked well	Exceeded budget on viral video campaign
Speed: Results, measurement analysis	Surveys returned quickly	Didn't gather enough qualitative information from customer focus group immediately after the event

Building upon this type of quick-and-easy tracking grid, you could then create additional, more detailed categories of items to assess. There are a multitude of different marketing activities and tactics to use. In the following paragraphs I've described five of the most common. I've also included a few suggestions about how to measure the effectiveness of each one and what questions to ask to ensure you're getting the right results for your marketing. When it comes to evaluating your programs, it's easy to rely solely on the numbers and focus on just the quantitative results. But they never give you the full picture. You have to dig deeper, beyond just the surface-level statistics, to get to the real answers. And it doesn't take too much extra effort to infuse your analysis process with a few qualifying questions to support your efforts. In case it's helpful, you might want to refer back to Chapter 2, where I discussed the difference between qualitative and quantitative research.

1. Advertising

Starting with the basics, you need to determine if your ad ran when it should have and if it included all of the information you provided. Did people see it? And if so, what did they think of it? Beyond that, you've got to find out if it really worked for your business. People in the advertising world have different theories about how frequently to run ads and how often a person needs to be exposed to one before he or she will respond. This is true for print as well as online and broadcast advertisements. The fastest way for you to measure the effectiveness of your ad campaign is to include a clear call to action. This is information you include to get people to do what you want them to do: call you, e-mail you, or visit your Website. More importantly, it gives you something specific you can measure.

This is one of the values of using print coupons as part of your marketing mix or considering doing a campaign through an online service such as Groupon. You can instantly see the effectiveness of your program with Groupon, not only in the number of people who originally bought the coupon, but also the number of people who actually used it. And from there, you can further evaluate if those people continue to come back and spend money with you or if they were just a one-Groupon wonder. That's a call to action that gives you a way to measure and determine the effectiveness of the effort and whether you should be doing it again in the future. Is there a call to action in your ad? Did people call you or come in? You need to know if your ad worked to meet—or, better yet, exceed—your goals, and impacted people's thinking and/or behavior as you had intended.

2. Events

When it comes to events, it's easy to slip into the habit of just counting the number of people who attended. For example, you hope to get 100 people to your fundraisers. This is what's often informally called the "butts in seats" method of assessment. It's all about quantity. I want to encourage you to dig deeper than that. Take a closer look at *who* actually filled those chairs. Were they the type of people you needed to be there? In the case of a fundraiser, were they people with big checkbooks who made large donations and helped you meet your goal? Beyond that, did the attendees take away the information and messages you intended to share? How do you know? Was there a call to action? If you did your strategic work up front, you'll know if you have the right results the minute the bidding begins.

3. Social Media

Social media campaigns are treated similarly to events in that people tend to base success only on looking at the numbers. This comes across in reports that only show how many tweets were sent and the number of people retweeting you. Again, dig deeper and assess who is doing the retweeting and read the context of those tweets. Were the original tweets copied verbatim or was something different communicated? And who are the people following you on Twitter, friending you on Facebook, and pinning you on Pinterest? Are they the people you want, or should you go after others? As I noted in the Kony example, social media activities have the power to spread information like wildfire, but sometimes you need to contain the heat.

4. PR

The effectiveness of media relations was historically measured in column inches: If your new mobile app was mentioned in a *Wired* magazine story that was three column inches long, the value of that article would be roughly equivalent to the cost of an advertisement of the same size in the publication. But we've come a long way since those days. Just as I've suggested for events and social media, it's good to look beyond the length to evaluate the effectiveness of your PR activities. If you sent a release out, did the kind of media you wanted to target pick it up? If so, did they print your story verbatim or go with a different news angle?

After an interview, did the reporter include your spokesperson's key messages in the news report? Did the media outlet use the supplemental materials you provided, such as graphics, photos, or video? As you can see, this isn't just about quantitative analysis anymore; it's all about the quality of the coverage. Did they include a link to your Website? Did people click on it? Are customers letting you know in some way that they saw, read, or heard your news story, and are they even the right people you wanted to reach? These are all important questions you need to ask to evaluate whether your PR worked.

5. Direct Mail

It doesn't matter if you send a postcard through snail mail or e-mail a newsletter, you have to be objective and determine if it was effective. It can feel as though you've reached success when you send e-newsletters to 10,000 people or finally pass out the last box of 500 fliers. But you don't really know until you push beyond those initial numbers. In the case of the e-newsletter, you do need to know how many people read it and clicked through. Many organizations use tools such as MailChimp or Constant Contact to measure and analyze how their customers are interacting with e-mail content. But did they like the content? Did they share it with anyone? Did any of them end up spending time on your Website and making a purchase? How do you know? Are you using Google Analytics or some other tool to gather this information? Do you need to quickly pull together a focus group to see if they would prefer you used a different template or a completely different method of marketing? These are all valuable questions to ask.

EVENT SURVEYS

In addition to gathering information in a postmortem group meeting, it can be helpful in some situations to conduct anonymous surveys. These work especially well following a business transaction, such as after completing a sale or delivering a service. They are just as effective for events and other types of marketing campaigns. The surveys can be sent to the people directly involved in planning and conducting the marketing activities, as well as participating customers, partners, and other external audiences.

Kerry Lehto, owner of KL Communications, Inc., has created and tabulated more than half a million event surveys in the past 17 years. With his graduate school training in numerical analysis and experience with Fortune-500 companies and private events of all sizes, he knows how to get the right results quickly, and the best way to assess the results. Here are a few top-level pointers from Kerry, especially if you're considering doing a survey after an event:

1. **Keep it short.** Whatever you do, don't make your survey too long. Unless someone is anxious to give feedback (and most people aren't), they tire easily from having to answer too many questions. This applies to both hard copy and online surveys.

2. **Give them something in return.** If you want responses, give the participant some incentive to return the survey, whether it's a small, in-person gift or an online coupon or discount. Or tell them they're automatically entered into a raffle or sweepstakes if they return the survey. This is especially effective if you need an authentic way to follow up with attendees after an event. Even if they don't win the prize, you can offer them a discount on your Website. This simple communication keeps them in the loop for future events and also keeps your company top of mind.

3. **Ask plenty of qualitative questions with write-in responses.**
    These might include questions such as, "What did you like most
    about attending this event, and why?," and "What could we do to
    improve this event next year?," and so on. You could be really spe-
    cific and ask that last question as, "What one thing could we do to
    improve this event next year, and why?" These types of open-ended
    questions provide you with extremely valuable feedback you can't
    get from a simple yes-or-no answer.

4. **Overall event questions.** Consider asking questions to help you
    gather feedback on aspects of the event beyond the content pre-
    sented. You can ask questions about logistics (event venue, events
    staff, meals, and so on), speakers (rate them on performance and
    content), networking opportunities, length of the event, and many
    more topics of your choosing.

5. **Repeated questions from previous surveys.** This is where it really
    gets interesting. It's great to ask questions to find out how the event
    compares to similar events held previously, or questions regarding
    the respondents' perceptions of the company holding the event.
    Asking these questions at every related event allows you to see how
    your customers perceive you, and how the current event compares
    to past events. It's vital to know how you're measuring up, what you
    need to change to do better, and what you need to keep doing at
    the event to keep your attendees happy and coming back for more.

THE FINAL ASSESSMENT

Now comes the time to do your final assessment. This is where you
review your plan and all of your activities, evaluate the results, and see if
you made the grade. This is the tricky part and where you *really* need to be
honest. How did you do? Do you get an A+? Or were you more of a B-? I
hope all of your hard work didn't end in an F—especially after reading this
book! But if that's the case, it's time to build upon that experience, roll up
your sleeves, and start moving your marketing forward again.

AMERICAN EXPRESS

An excellent example of a company that put all of this into play and quickly gathered valuable results from a comprehensive marketing campaign involving multiple activities and events is American Express. Thanks to the digital marketplace, the company faced new challenges as online financial service providers such as PayPal crept into its customer base. In an effort to avoid becoming "your grandfather's credit card," the company made a strategic decision to enter the digital-payment space with an innovative new product: Serve.[9] With the benefits of a credit card, debit card, and an online payment service rolled into one, Serve was designed to reach a new type of American Express customer. This included people who didn't already have credit or debit cards, such as people who used cash as their main form of payment, and a younger demographic used to using smart phones for all transactions. For this reason, the product needed to be tested, and because the competitive landscape was expanding rapidly, the testing needed to be done quickly.

From the start, American Express took a guerilla approach to marketing Serve and decided to create a strategic test-pilot campaign. Even for such a global corporation, initial budgets were limited and timelines tight until the product's market had been proven. But the company pulled its resources together and built upon its strengths, and in just a few weeks came up with a streamlined action plan.

Eugene, Oregon, was chosen as the test city for several reasons. Because of the presence of the University of Oregon, a large group of young people could be reached easily. Eugene is on the West Coast, with Microsoft to the north and Apple to the south, so there was a good chance that youth would be tech-savvy. Lastly, Eugene is known as an alternative city or hippie town, with a skeptical attitude toward corporations. Of all places, Eugene would be the right environment to get honest feedback about an offering such as Serve.

Within a few weeks, American Express was able to leverage its resources, build upon its strengths, and quickly create authentic relationships in the local community. Everyone from the Greenhill Humane Society to the university's Lundquist College of Business was willing to get involved and help the company test its new platform. Once those key community relationships were in place, the marketing activities began, including a Facebook campaign, media outreach, radio ads and promotions, and activities with university students.

One specific marketing program was created with the Eugene Saturday Market, the oldest weekly open-air crafts market in the United States, in operation since 1970. American Express teamed up with the market's management to reach more than 25 local vendors and partnered with them to help test Serve in their individual booths. Offering small cash incentives to both merchants and customers helped create new Serve accounts. The program lasted four weeks and gave American Express a perfect opportunity to demonstrate the product and get it onto mobile phones in the hands of potential customers.

The company gained tremendous value from this quick test pilot. In just a few months, it gave American Express an immediate snapshot of real-world scenarios and feedback on how people were using the product. It also allowed company management to get face-to-face responses from people on the street. By swiftly testing its new product and marketing messages with the public as well as the media and bloggers, American Express was able to learn what worked and what didn't and significantly improve future versions of its new payment method.

⮕　⮕　⮕

In this chapter, you've seen the importance of finding quick ways to measure the effectiveness of your marketing. Keeping track of your progress every step of the way is key, as is doing a comprehensive assessment as soon as the project is completed. Strike while the iron is hot; a swift analysis will ensure you capture your clearest, most helpful observations. This process is easy to skip, but focusing on it is crucial to the success of your marketing.

When wrapping up and analyzing a project, I'm a big believer in the messaging sandwich approach. Start with the good: What went well? Who needs kudos? Then, put on your objective hat and be open to constructive feedback that could help improve your future efforts. What could've gone better? What caught you by surprise? What did you forget? And what lessons were learned? Then wrap up the results session with a final dose of the good stuff: When do we celebrate?

The Marketing Mindset

Take a few minutes to reflect on what you've read in this chapter and answer the following questions:

1. What are some examples of current marketing activities you need to assess?

2. What is a fast and effective way for you to measure the results of one of your marketing campaigns?

3. Are you clear about the return on investment you need to make?

4. Is it important for you to factor in a return on impact, as well? Why or why not?

5. Does it make sense for you to conduct a survey to quickly evaluate a marketing program?

CONCLUSION

Keep Your Momentum

THANK YOU FOR READING my book. I hope the time you've invested is proving valuable and that you found the information and stories interesting and helpful. I wrote the book to help give you the fuel you need to move forward. I don't expect you to use every idea I've given you, but I hope most of them resonated with you on some level, either validating your original thinking or giving you a new perspective to consider.

Whether you manage your own business, work in a large corporation, attend college, run a nonprofit, or land somewhere in between, I hope you now know that marketing, when done with intention, has the potential to transform your organization and move you forward toward your vision. You just need to apply the five keys—strategy, story, strength, simplicity, and speed—to produce great results.

When I speak to audiences and deliver seminars on the concepts I've shared here with you, most people are immediately inspired to begin using their marketing in new ways. They want to start right away by revamping their Website to ensure it connects with customers, or they want to find partners who can help contribute content to their blog.

Other people are similarly full of ideas, but for whatever reason still need a hand. Typically, they return to their desk, become consumed with the day-to-day business, and marketing falls to the bottom of their to-do list. I don't want this to happen to you. I want you to take that first step to move your marketing forward.

As I've shown you, it doesn't have to be complicated, time-consuming, or expensive. Just get out there and try. Start with your strategy and spend some time thinking about what you really need to accomplish. Kick around some ideas about your unique brand and story and who needs to hear more about it. Try strengthening your efforts by doing more with your customers, teaming up with a partner, or sharing your news with the media. Along the way, keep your plan and process simple. And finally, don't overthink it. It doesn't need to be perfect; just get out there and do it. Use every resource you've got and watch for what works and what doesn't. Tweak along the way until you start getting the right results.

I said at the very start of the book that marketing isn't always linear. Every organization has to find the unique combination of marketing actions that will work for its particular situation. In some ways, it's more of an art form than a science. Effective marketing is the ability to share a message with an intended audience and get the right result. That could take the form of a podcast or a new page on your Website. You won't know until you try.

If you need a nudge to get started or support along the way, I hope you'll visit my Website. You'll find free templates and examples, as well as other resources and multimedia tools such as Marketing Minute videos with ideas and tips. And if you're already benefiting from the information in this book, I'd love to hear from you—I would be happy to share your success story on my blog or in keynotes and lectures.

I wish you nothing but success, however you define it.

Whitney Keyes
whitney@whitneykeyes.com
WhitneyKeyes.com/Propel

Notes

Note: All Websites were accessed May–June 2012.

INTRODUCTION

1. Carr, Austin. "Groupon Says Super Bowl Ads 'Execution Was Off,' Pulls Them From TV, YouTube." *Fast Company*, February 11, 2011. *www.fastcompany.com/1726655/ groupon-crispin-porter-bogusky-pulls-controversial-super-bowl-ads.*

2. Wheaton, Ken. "Groupon Pulls Controversial Super Bowl Ads." *AdAgeBLOGS*, February 11, 2011. *http://adage.com/article/adages/ groupon-pulls-controversial-super-bowl-ads/148839/.*

3. Longley, Robert. "Why Small Businesses Fail: SBA." *About. com*, US Government Info. *http://usgovinfo.about.com/od/ smallbusiness/a/whybusfail.htm.*

4. Arthur, Lisa. "CMOs Optimistic, But Social Media Disconnect Remains." Forbes.com, April 6, 2011. *www.forbes.com/sites/lisaarthur/2011/04/06/cmos-optimistic-but-social-media-disconnect-remains.*

5. James, Blaise, and Jim Asplund. "Social Media: The Three Big Myths." *Gallup Business Journal. http://gmj.gallup.com/content/148694/social-media-three-big-myths.aspx.*

6. American Marketing Association Website: marketingpower. *www.marketingpower.com/Pages/default.aspx.*

CHAPTER 1

1. Bernhard, Kent, Jr. "Recession Brought a Small-Business Boom." Portfolio.com, May 20, 2011. *www.portfolio.com/views/blogs/resources/2011/05/20/number-of-small-businesses-rose-since-recession.*

2. Covey, Stephen R., A. Roger Merrill, and Rebecca R. Merrill. *First Things First.* New York: The Free Press, 2003, pp. 103–104.

3. Whole Foods Market. "Sustainability and Our Future." *www.wholefoodsmarket.com/company/sustainability.php.*

4. Medley, Kate. "Gaia Herbs." *Whole Story: The Official Whole Foods Markets Blog,* March 8, 2012. *http://blog.wholefoodsmarket.com/2012/03/gaia-herbs-2/.*

5. "What Is an Objective?" ClearHorizon.com. *www.clearhorizon.com.au/discussion/what-is-an-objective.*

6. "SMART criteria." Wikipedia. *http://en.wikipedia.org/wiki/SMART_criteria.*

7. Balanced Scorecard Institute. *www.balancedscorecard.org.*

CHAPTER 2

1. "SWOT ANALYSIS." Reference for Business, *Encyclopedia of Business,* 2nd ed. *www.referenceforbusiness.com/management/Pr-Sa/SWOT-Analysis.html#ixzz1inww0JSE.*

2. "Airbnb at a Glance." *www.airbnb.com/home/press.*

3. Lynley, Matt. "Here's Why I Will Never Use Airbnb Again." *Business Insider*, Novermber 21, 2011. *www.businessinsider.com/ heres-why-i-will-never-use-airbnb-again-2011-11.*

CHAPTER 3

1. Bogenrief, Margaret. "How Gap Came Apart at the Seams." *Business Insider*, January 3, 2012. *http://articles.businessinsider.com/2012-01-03/ strategy/30582910_1_gap-sales-gap-shares-apparel#ixzz1pPDs6Jhw.*

2. Walker, Alissa. "Gap on Disastrous New Logo : We're Open to Other Ideas." Fast Company Co.DESIGN. *www.fastcodesign. com/1662452/gap-on-disastrous-new-logo-were-open-to-other-ideas.*

3. Halliday, Josh. "Gap Scraps Logo Redesign After Protests on Facebook and Twitter." *The Guardian*, October 12, 2010. *www. guardian.co.uk/media/2010/oct/12/gap-logo-redesign.*

4. Hampp, Andrew. "Gap to Scrap New Logo, Return to Old Design." *AdvertisingAge*, October 11, 2010. *http://adage.com/ article/news/gap-scrap-logo-return-design/146417/.*

5. "Guidelines for Use of the Twitter Trademark." Twitter.com. *https://support.twitter.com/entries/77641.*

6. "MSN Butterfly Squad Nationwide Tour Takes Flight." *Microsoft News Center*, February 13, 2003. *www.microsoft.com/presspass/ press/2003/feb03/02-13butterflytourpr.mspx.*

7. Dunlap, David W. "City Officials Tell Microsoft to Get Its Butterfly Decals out of Town." *The New York Times*, October 25, 2002. *www.nytimes.com/2002/10/25/nyregion/city-officials-tell-microsoft-to-get-its-butterfly-decals-out-of-town.html.*

8. "Microsoft Ruling Overturned." *The Washington Post* Business: Microsoft. *www.washingtonpost.com/wp-dyn/business/specials/ microsofttrial/index.html.*

9. "About Microsoft." Microsoft: Our Mission. *www.microsoft.com/ about/en/us/default.aspx.*

10. Microsoft Corporate Citizenship. *www.microsoft.com/hk/ citizenship/english.*

CHAPTER 4

1. "History of Cocoa." World Cocoa Foundation. *www. worldcocoafoundation.org/learn-about-cocoa/history-of-cocoa.html.*

2. "Hershey's History." Hershey's. *www.thehersheycompany.com/about-hershey/our-story/hersheys-history.aspx.*

3. Cowtown Candy Company. www.cowtowncandy.com/CowtownCandy/About_Cowtown_Candy.html.

CHAPTER 5

1. "How to Cut Through Marketing Clutter." Marketing Made Simple. *www.marketing-made-simple.com/articles/promotional-clutter.htm#axzz1njtUMguF.*

2. Rieck, Dean. "A Secret Look at How People Read Your Direct Mail." Direct Creative, 2001. *www.directcreative.com/a-secret-look-at-how-people-read-your-direct-mail.html.*

CHAPTER 6

1. Alkatib, Sukaynah. "The Taste of Africa at Fusion Restaurant." *The Namibian,* August 30, 2010. *www.namibian.com.na/index.php?id=28&tx_ttnews[tt_news]=71838&no_cache=1.*

CHAPTER 7

1. McIlroy, Thad. "The Future of Magazines." The Future of Publishing, August 1, 2011. *http://thefutureofpublishing.com/industries/the-future-of-magazines/#how_many_magazines.*

CHAPTER 8

1. Empson, Rip. "Vimeo Launches Audiosocket-Powered Music Store to Bring Tunes to Video." TechCrunch.com, September 21, 2011. *http://techcrunch.com/2011/09/21/vimeo-launches-audiosocket-powered-music-store-to-bring-tunes-to-video.*

CHAPTER 9

1. "Procter & Gamble." Wikipedia.org. *http://en.wikipedia.org/wiki/ Procter_%26_Gamble.*

CHAPTER 10

1. Sharkey, Joe. "A Bonanza for Airlines as Taxes End." *The New York Times,* July 25, 2011. *www.nytimes.com/2011/07/26/business/ airlines-raise-fares-as-federal-taxes-expire.html.*

2. Invisiblechildreninc. "Kony 2012: Invisible Children." YouTube. com, March 5, 2012. *www.youtube.com/watch?v=Y4MnpzG5Sqc.*

3. bduncan. "Rihanna, Justin Bieber, Nathan Sykes and More Get Behind the Kony 2012 Campaign." SugarScape.com, March 8, 2012. *www.sugarscape.com/main-topics/celebrities/702189/ rihanna-justin-bieber-and-more-get-behind-kony-2012-campaign.*

4. Finlayson, Ariana. "Kony 2012 Documentary Sparks Support from Diddy, Kim Kardashian, Rihanna, Other Celebs." *Us Magazine,* March 8, 2012. *www.usmagazine.com/celebrity-news/ news/kony-2012-documentary-sparks-support-from-diddy-kim- kardashian-rihanna-other-celebs-201283.*

5. Invisible Children Official Store. Kony 2012 Action Kit. *http:// invisiblechildrenstore.myshopify.com/products/kony-kit.*

6. Basu, Moni. "As Criticism Surfaces, 'KONY 2012' Gains Momentum Faster Than Susan Boyle." CNN.com, March 9, 2012. *http://articles.cnn.com/2012-03-09/africa/world_africa_ uganda-viral-video_1_joseph-kony-invisible-children-lord-s- resistance-army?_s=PM:AFRICA.*

7. Bell, Melissa. "Invisible Children Co-Founder Jason Russell Hospitalized After Public Breakdown." *The Washington Post* blogPOST, March 16, 2012. *www.washingtonpost.com/blogs/ blogpost/post/invisible-children-co-founder-jason-russell-reportedly- arrested/2012/03/16/gIQAuBl5GS_blog.html?tid=pm_pop.*

8. Carroll, Rory. "Kony 2012 Cover the Night Fails to Move from the Internet to the Streets." *The Guardian,* April 21, 2012. *www.guardian.co.uk/world/2012/apr/21/ kony-2012-campaign-uganda-warlord.*

9. "American Express Announces Serve(SM), the Next Generation Digital Payment Platform." American Express News: Press Release, March 28, 2011. *http://about.americanexpress.com/news/ pr/2011/serve.aspx.*

Index

About the Author

WHITNEY KEYES IS AN international speaker, marketing expert, and professor of strategic communications. For more than 20 years, she has helped organizations and individuals be more successful. Whitney has worked as a senior Microsoft manager, a strategic advisor for American Express, and a marketing consultant to thousands of businesses around the world. She has also worked for the U.S. Department of State to empower women entrepreneurs in Malaysia, Kenya, and Namibia.

While at Microsoft, Whitney managed global marketing campaigns, including the launch of Office 2000, an $8-billion business, and helped create the company's primary philanthropy program, Unlimited Potential. Today, Whitney serves as a fellow for the Center for Strategic Communications at Seattle University and guest lectures for the University of Washington and other academic institutions. She also manages a consulting practice, delivers keynotes, and facilitates workshops for national organizations, including the Small Business Administration. Whitney writes for business publications and produces content for the *Seattle Post-Intelligencer*'s Biz Bite Blog. Whitney lives in Seattle, Washington, and can be reached through her website at WhitneyKeyes.com.

SPEAKING AND EVENTS

Trying to get more customers through your door or to your Website? Need to get your name in the news? Want more information on how to use marketing to move your business forward and get results quickly? Whitney Keyes is available as a speaker to deliver engaging keynote presentations and conferences around the world. She has spoken to businesswomen in Malaysia and college students in Africa. She is experienced in delivering talks and facilitating discussions that help individuals and organizations get to the next level, be it at a corporate event or a professional conference.

Whitney's clients range from the U.S. State Department to the Washington State Bar Association. Her sessions are always customized to meet the needs of each group and support the goals of the event planner. She uses real-world examples and case studies, and her fast-paced presentation style keeps things interesting and interactive. Her approach blends traditional marketing and PR strategies with current tools such as viral YouTube videos, Twitter, and Pinterest. Each presentation delivers valuable, actionable information and leaves participants informed, inspired, and ready to move forward.

Here are just a few things some of her previous clients have had to say about her programs:

"We were absolutely thrilled with your program!" —Nick Papp, U.S. Embassy, Malaysia

"Whitney, your enthusiasm was infectious, and we all learned a lot from your expertise and insights." —John Smilgin, NW Entrepreneur Think Tank

"Whitney's presentation received the highest rating from 95 percent of all event attendees. She is articulate, entertaining, engaging, and able to clearly communicate complicated information." —Matthew Price, Microsoft

"Whitney, you are amazing. Such clear thinking and strategies." —Jena Cane, Guiding Lights

"Whitney was so open and interested, and we really appreciated hearing about her experiences. Her ability to compare Kenyan female entrepreneurs to other populations she's worked with was particularly useful." —Grace Hopewell, ECON, Africa

"Almost 90 percent of our event participants said they were very likely to use the information Whitney shared in her seminar in their businesses." —Christine Clifford, City of Tacoma

"Our marketing event was a success, thanks to having Whitney as the speaker!" —Kelly Sharples, NWEM

"Whitney's presentations are always infused with real-life experiences and creative ideas. We bring her back as a speaker year after year." —Sherry Mina, Small Business Administration

Whitney's topics and themes include:

⟶ **Strategy:** Vision, goals, leadership, corporate social responsibility, social entrepreneurism

⟶ **Story:** Branding, value, target market, customer segments, niches

⟶ **Strength:** Customers, partnerships, traditional and social media, other opinion influencers

⟶ **Simplicity:** Action planning, maximizing resources

⟶ **Speed:** Quickly getting the right results, measurement and evaluation, success

Contact Whitney directly for more information about her speaking services and availability for your next event at WhitneyKeyes.com.